THIS BOOK
BELONGS TO

....

....

I can't tell you how grateful I am that you decided to read my book. My most heartfelt thanks that you took time out of your life to choose my work and I hope you find benefit within these pages.

There are so many books available today that offer similar content so that makes it even more humbling that you decided to buying mine.

Tell me what you thought! I am eager to hear your opinion and ideas on what you read as are others who are looking for a good book to buy. Leave a review on Amazon.com so others can benefit from your wisdom!

With much thanks.

Copyright

All rights reserved. No part of this publication may be reproduced, stored in a retrieval system, or transmitted in any form or by any means, electronic, mechanical, photocopying, recording or otherwise, without the prior written permission of the Publisher.

Table of Contents

SUMMARY

    INTRODUCTION TO STUMPWORK EMBROIDERY   27

    CHAPTER ONE   27

        EMBROIDER ON LEATHER   27

        REQUIREMENTS   28

        GUIDELINES   30

            MARK THE PATTERN ON THE LEATHER   31

            EMBROIDER THROUGH THE LEATHER   34

            MEASURE AND MARK THE HOLES FOR THE SIDE SEAMS   34

            SEW THE SIDES OF THE CARD CASE TOGETHER   35

    CHAPTER TWO   39

        DIY EMBROIDERED BARGELLO   39

        BRIEF HISTORY ABOUT BARGELLO   40

        REQUIREMENTS   41

        GUIDELINES   41

    CHAPTER THREE   53

        DIY EMBROIDERED SWEATER   53

        WHAT YOU WILL REQUIRE   55

        GUIDELINES FOR THE SWEATER   56

    CHAPTER FOUR   60

        DIY SWEDISH HUCK EMBROIDERY   61

        SUPPLIES FOR HUCK EMBROIDERY   62

        GUIDELINES   65

    CHAPTER FIVE   70

        DIY CANDLEWICK EMBROIDERY   70

        WHAT YOU WILL REQUIRE   72

        INSTRUCTIONS   72

    CHAPTER SIX   77

        EMBROIDERED THROW PILLOW   78

        SUPPLIES FOR THE EMBROIDERED THROW PILLOW   78

        EMBROIDERED PILLOW: A STEP-BY-STEP TUTORIAL   79

    CHAPTER SEVEN   86

DIY EMBROIDERED MAGNETS	86
MATERIALS	87
GUIDELINES	89

SUMMARY

What is The Stumpwork Embroidery: The Stumpwork Embroidery is a unique and intricate form of embroidery that originated in the 17th century. It is characterized by its three-dimensional and raised elements, which are created by padding and shaping the fabric with various materials such as felt, wire, or cotton. This technique gives the embroidery a sculptural quality, making it stand out from other forms of embroidery.

The Stumpwork Embroidery often features a combination of different stitches, such as satin stitch, chain stitch, and French knots, to create intricate details and textures. These stitches are used to embellish the raised elements and add depth and dimension to the design. The embroidery can depict a wide range of subjects, including flowers, animals, figures, and landscapes.

One of the key features of The Stumpwork Embroidery is the use of appliqué, where pieces of fabric or other materials are attached to the base fabric to create specific shapes or designs. This technique allows for greater flexibility and creativity in the embroidery, as different fabrics can be used to achieve different effects.

Another important aspect of The Stumpwork Embroidery is the use of wire to create delicate and realistic shapes. The wire is often used to create the stems of flowers, the wings of birds, or the limbs of figures. It is carefully shaped and stitched onto the fabric, giving the embroidery a lifelike quality.

The Stumpwork Embroidery requires a high level of skill and precision, as the three-dimensional elements need to be carefully constructed and attached to the fabric. It is a time-consuming process that requires patience and attention to detail. However, the end result is a stunning piece of art that showcases the creativity and craftsmanship of the embroiderer.

Today, The Stumpwork Embroidery continues to be practiced by skilled artisans and is highly regarded in the world of embroidery. It is often used to create decorative pieces, such as wall hangings, cushions, and framed artworks. The intricate details and three-dimensional elements make it a popular choice for those looking to add a touch of elegance and sophistication to their home decor.

In conclusion, The Stumpwork Embroidery is a unique and intricate form of embroidery that combines three-dimensional elements, appliqué, and wirework to create stunning and lifelike designs. It requires a high level of skill and precision, but the end result is a beautiful piece of art that showcases the creativity and craftsmanship of the embroiderer.

Why Stumpwork Embroidery Is Unique: Stumpwork embroidery is a unique and intricate form of embroidery that has been practiced for centuries. It is characterized by its three-dimensional and raised elements, which give the artwork a stunning and lifelike appearance. This technique involves creating padded shapes and figures using various materials such as felt, wire, and fabric, and then stitching them onto the fabric base.

One of the reasons why stumpwork embroidery is so unique is its ability to create a sense of depth and dimension in the artwork. By using padding and raised elements, the artist can make certain parts of the design stand out, giving it a three-dimensional effect. This adds a level of realism and visual interest that is not typically seen in other forms of embroidery.

Another aspect that sets stumpwork embroidery apart is the level of skill and precision required to create these intricate designs. The artist must have a deep understanding of embroidery techniques and be able to manipulate the materials to achieve the desired effect. This includes shaping the padding, attaching it securely to the fabric, and carefully stitching the details to bring the design to life. It is a labor-intensive process that requires patience, attention to detail, and a steady hand.

Furthermore, stumpwork embroidery offers a wide range of creative possibilities. Artists can create a variety of subjects, from flowers and animals to people and landscapes. The raised elements allow for a greater level of detail and complexity in the design, making it possible to capture even the smallest nuances and textures. This versatility allows artists to express their creativity and bring their imagination to life through their needlework.

Additionally, stumpwork embroidery has a rich history and cultural significance. It has been practiced in various cultures around the world, each with its own unique style and techniques. For example, in Elizabethan England, stumpwork embroidery was used to create elaborate and decorative motifs on clothing and accessories. In India, it was used to embellish textiles and create intricate designs for ceremonial purposes. This historical context adds depth and meaning to the art form, making it even more special and valuable.

In conclusion, stumpwork embroidery is a truly unique and remarkable form of art. Its ability to create three-dimensional and lifelike designs, the level of skill and precision required, the creative possibilities it offers, and its rich history and cultural significance all contribute to its uniqueness. Whether you are an artist or an admirer of embroidery, stumpwork embroidery is sure to captivate and inspire with its beauty and intricacy.

Understanding the Basics of Stumpwork Embroidery: Stumpwork embroidery is a unique and intricate form of embroidery that involves creating three-dimensional designs on fabric. It is a technique that has been practiced for centuries and continues to be popular among embroidery enthusiasts today. In order to understand the basics of stumpwork embroidery, it is important to familiarize oneself with the materials, techniques, and designs commonly used in this art form.

One of the key elements of stumpwork embroidery is the use of padding. Padding is the process of adding layers of material, such as felt or cotton, underneath the embroidery stitches to create a raised effect. This technique allows for the creation of three-dimensional shapes and designs, giving stumpwork embroidery its distinctive look. The padding can be done using various methods, such as needle weaving or layering, depending on the desired effect.

Another important aspect of stumpwork embroidery is the use of wire. Wire is often used to create the structural framework for the three-dimensional elements in the design. It can be shaped and manipulated to form the desired shape, such as petals, leaves, or even figures. The wire is then covered with embroidery stitches to blend it seamlessly with the rest of the design. This combination of wire and embroidery creates a stunning effect that adds depth and dimension to the finished piece.

In addition to padding and wire, stumpwork embroidery often incorporates other techniques and materials to enhance the overall design. For example, beads, sequins, and metallic threads are commonly used to add sparkle and texture to the embroidery. These embellishments can be stitched onto the fabric or attached using other methods, such as glue or wire wrapping. The use of these additional materials allows for endless possibilities in creating unique and eye-catching stumpwork designs.

When it comes to the actual stitching techniques used in stumpwork embroidery, there are several to choose from. Some of the most commonly used stitches include satin stitch, long and short stitch, and couching. These stitches are used to fill in the design and create the desired texture and shape. It is important to have a good understanding of these stitches and how they can be combined to achieve different effects in stumpwork embroidery.

As for the designs themselves, stumpwork embroidery offers a wide range of possibilities. From floral motifs to animals, figures, and even landscapes, the options are virtually limitless. Many embroidery enthusiasts enjoy creating their own designs, while others prefer to use pre-drawn patterns or kits.

The History and Evolution of Stumpwork: Stumpwork is a form of embroidery that has a rich history and has evolved over time to become a highly intricate and decorative art form. Its origins can be traced back to the 17th century in England, where it was initially used to create three-dimensional motifs on clothing and accessories.

The term "stumpwork" is believed to have originated from the practice of using a wooden stump as a base for creating raised and padded elements in the embroidery. This technique allowed for the creation of lifelike and realistic designs, as well as the incorporation of various materials such as beads, sequins, and metal threads.

During the 17th and 18th centuries, stumpwork gained popularity among the upper classes in England and Europe. It was often used to embellish clothing, particularly on garments worn for special occasions such as weddings and formal events. The intricate and detailed nature of stumpwork made it a symbol of wealth and status, as it required skilled artisans to create these elaborate designs.

As time went on, stumpwork began to incorporate more complex techniques and designs. In the 19th century, the art form saw a resurgence in popularity with the rise of the Arts and Crafts movement. Artists and designers began experimenting with new materials and techniques, pushing the boundaries of what could be achieved with stumpwork.

In the 20th century, stumpwork continued to evolve and adapt to changing artistic trends. It became more accessible to a wider audience, with the introduction of kits and patterns that allowed hobbyists to try their hand at this intricate embroidery technique. Stumpwork also began to be used in contemporary art and fashion, with artists and designers incorporating it into their work to create unique and visually stunning pieces.

Today, stumpwork remains a popular form of embroidery, with dedicated artisans and enthusiasts keeping the tradition alive. It is often used to create decorative pieces such as framed artwork, jewelry, and accessories. The techniques and materials used in stumpwork have also expanded, with artists incorporating modern elements such as digital embroidery and unconventional materials to create innovative and contemporary designs.

The history and evolution of stumpwork showcase its enduring appeal and versatility as an art form. From its humble beginnings as a technique to create raised motifs on clothing, stumpwork has grown into a highly intricate and decorative embroidery style that continues to captivate and inspire artists and enthusiasts around the world.

Essential Tools and Supplies of Stumpwork Embroidery: Stumpwork embroidery is a unique and intricate form of embroidery that involves creating three-dimensional designs on fabric. To successfully create stunning stumpwork pieces, it is essential to have the right tools and supplies at hand. These tools and supplies not only make the embroidery process easier but also help in achieving the desired results.

One of the most important tools for stumpwork embroidery is a good quality embroidery hoop. The hoop holds the fabric taut, allowing for precise stitching and preventing any puckering or distortion. It is recommended to use a hoop that is slightly larger than the design area to provide enough working space.

Embroidery needles are another essential tool for stumpwork embroidery. These needles come in various sizes and shapes, each serving a specific purpose. For stumpwork, it is recommended to have a selection of sharp and blunt-ended needles. Sharp needles are used for fine details and precise stitching, while blunt needles are used for padding and creating raised elements.

A pair of sharp embroidery scissors is a must-have for stumpwork embroidery. These scissors are used for cutting threads, trimming fabric, and snipping away excess materials. It is important to keep the scissors sharp to ensure clean and precise cuts.

A variety of threads and yarns are required for stumpwork embroidery. Silk threads, cotton threads, and metallic threads are commonly used to create different textures and effects. It is advisable to have a range of colors and thicknesses to add depth and dimension to the design. Additionally, using specialized threads like wire threads or braids can help in creating raised elements and adding a touch of sparkle to the embroidery.

To create the three-dimensional effect in stumpwork embroidery, padding materials are essential. These materials include felt, cotton batting, or foam. They are used to build up the design and create raised areas. The padding materials are cut into the desired shape and stitched onto the fabric before being covered with embroidery stitches.

In addition to the basic tools and supplies, there are some optional tools that can enhance the stumpwork embroidery experience. These include a lightbox for tracing designs onto fabric, a magnifying glass for working on intricate details, and a thimble to protect the finger while stitching.

In conclusion, stumpwork embroidery requires a range of tools and supplies to achieve the desired results. From embroidery hoops and needles to threads and padding materials, each item plays a crucial role in creating stunning three-dimensional designs.

Reading Stumpwork Embroidery Patterns: Reading Stumpwork Embroidery Patterns is a comprehensive guide that provides detailed instructions and tips on how to effectively read and interpret stumpwork embroidery patterns. Stumpwork embroidery is a technique that involves creating three-dimensional designs using various materials such as wires, beads, and fabric. It is a highly intricate and artistic form of embroidery that requires a deep understanding of patterns and their symbols.

This guide begins by introducing the reader to the basics of stumpwork embroidery, including the materials and tools needed to get started. It then delves into the importance of understanding and interpreting patterns, as they serve as the blueprint for creating stunning stumpwork designs. The author explains how to decipher the symbols and instructions found in patterns, ensuring that readers can accurately translate them into their embroidery work.

One of the key aspects covered in this guide is the different types of stitches used in stumpwork embroidery. The author provides step-by-step instructions on how to execute each stitch, accompanied by detailed illustrations and photographs. This allows readers to not only understand the stitches conceptually but also visually see how they should be executed. Additionally, the guide offers tips and tricks for achieving clean and precise stitches, ensuring that the final embroidery piece is of the highest quality.

Furthermore, the guide explores the various techniques and methods used in stumpwork embroidery, such as padding, appliqué, and raised work. Each technique is explained in depth, with clear instructions on how to incorporate them into different patterns. The author also provides examples of finished stumpwork embroidery pieces, showcasing the versatility and beauty of this art form.

In addition to the technical aspects of stumpwork embroidery, this guide also delves into the creative side of the craft. It discusses how to choose colors and materials that complement each other, as well as how to add personal touches and variations to patterns. The author encourages readers to experiment and explore their own creativity, providing inspiration and guidance along the way.

Overall, Reading Stumpwork Embroidery Patterns is a valuable resource for both beginners and experienced embroiderers. It equips readers with the knowledge and skills needed to confidently read and interpret stumpwork embroidery patterns, allowing them to create stunning and intricate designs. Whether you are new to stumpwork embroidery or looking to enhance your existing skills, this guide is a must-have for any embroidery enthusiast.

The Foundation Stitches: Raised Work and Padding of Stumpwork Embroidery: Stumpwork embroidery is a technique that involves creating three-dimensional designs on fabric using various stitches and padding techniques. One of the key elements in stumpwork embroidery is the foundation stitches, which provide the base for building up the raised areas of the design.

The foundation stitches in stumpwork embroidery serve as a framework for the design and help create the desired shape and form. These stitches are typically worked on a separate piece of fabric, which is then attached to the main fabric using various techniques such as appliqué or couching.

There are several types of foundation stitches used in stumpwork embroidery, including satin stitch, long and short stitch, and split stitch. Satin stitch is commonly used for filling in large areas, while long and short stitch is used for creating smooth gradations of color. Split stitch is often used for outlining and adding fine details to the design.

In addition to the foundation stitches, padding is another important aspect of stumpwork embroidery. Padding is used to create the raised areas of the design and give it a three-dimensional effect. This can be achieved by layering different materials such as felt or cotton batting underneath the fabric and stitching over them to secure them in place.

The choice of padding materials depends on the desired effect and the thickness required. Thicker materials like felt can be used for creating more pronounced raised areas, while thinner materials like cotton batting can be used for subtle elevation.

Once the foundation stitches and padding are in place, the next step in stumpwork embroidery is to embellish the design with additional stitches and decorative elements. This can include adding beads, sequins, or even small objects like buttons or charms to enhance the overall look of the design.

Stumpwork embroidery allows for a great deal of creativity and experimentation, as there are no strict rules or limitations when it comes to design. Artists can create intricate and detailed designs or opt for more abstract and whimsical creations.

Overall, the foundation stitches and padding techniques in stumpwork embroidery play a crucial role in bringing the design to life and adding depth and dimension to the finished piece. With practice and patience, one can master these techniques and create stunning and unique stumpwork embroidery designs.

Building Dimension with Wire and Beads of Stumpwork Embroidery: Stumpwork embroidery is a unique and intricate form of embroidery that involves creating three-dimensional designs using wire and beads. One of the key elements in stumpwork embroidery is the use of building dimensions to add depth and texture to the design.

When working on a stumpwork embroidery project, the first step is to select a design or pattern. Once the design is chosen, the next step is to transfer it onto the fabric. This can be done by tracing the design onto the fabric or using a transfer pen or pencil. It is important to ensure that the design is accurately transferred onto the fabric, as this will serve as a guide for the placement of the wire and beads.

After the design is transferred, the next step is to start building dimensions. This involves using wire to create a framework for the three-dimensional elements of the design. The wire is carefully shaped and stitched onto the fabric, following the outline of the design. The wire serves as a support structure for the beads and other embellishments that will be added later.

Once the wire framework is in place, the next step is to add the beads. Beads of various sizes, shapes, and colors are carefully selected to enhance the design and add texture. The beads are stitched onto the fabric using a variety of techniques, such as couching, which involves stitching the beads onto the fabric using a separate thread.

The placement of the beads is crucial in creating the desired effect. They can be used to create highlights and shadows, as well as to add depth and dimension to the design. By strategically placing the beads, the embroidery artist can create a realistic and visually appealing three-dimensional effect.

In addition to wire and beads, other materials such as fabric scraps, ribbons, and sequins can also be used to add further dimension and texture to the design. These materials are carefully selected and stitched onto the fabric, complementing the wire and beadwork.

Stumpwork embroidery with building dimensions requires patience, precision, and attention to detail. It is a time-consuming process that requires careful planning and execution. However, the end result is a stunning piece of artwork that showcases the skill and creativity of the embroidery artist.

In conclusion, building dimensions with wire and beads is a key technique in stumpwork embroidery. It involves creating a wire framework and adding beads and other embellishments to create a three-dimensional effect. This technique requires careful planning, precision, and attention to detail, but the end result is a beautiful and unique piece of embroidery.

Mastering the Long and Short Stitch of Stumpwork Embroidery: In this comprehensive guide, we will delve into the art of stumpwork embroidery and explore the techniques of mastering the long and short stitch. Stumpwork embroidery is a three-dimensional form of embroidery that involves creating raised and padded areas on the fabric, giving the design a sculptural effect. The long and short stitch is a fundamental stitch in stumpwork embroidery that allows for smooth and seamless blending of colors and shading.

To begin our journey into mastering the long and short stitch of stumpwork embroidery, we will first explore the materials and tools needed for this technique. You will need a piece of fabric, preferably a tightly woven fabric such as linen or cotton, an embroidery hoop to hold the fabric taut, embroidery needles in various sizes, and a selection of embroidery threads in different colors. Additionally, you may require a pair of embroidery scissors, a thimble, and a needle threader for added convenience.

Once you have gathered your materials, we will move on to the preparatory steps before starting the long and short stitch. It is essential to transfer your design onto the fabric using a transfer method of your choice, such as tracing or using a water-soluble pen. This will serve as a guide for your stitching and ensure accurate placement of your design elements.

Now that we have our design transferred onto the fabric, we can begin practicing the long and short stitch. This stitch is commonly used for creating smooth color transitions and shading in stumpwork embroidery. To execute the long and short stitch, start by bringing your needle up through the fabric at the desired starting point of your stitch. Then, take a small stitch diagonally across the area you want to fill, ensuring that the stitch length is consistent.

Next, bring your needle back up through the fabric slightly to the right of the previous stitch, forming a slanted line. The length of this stitch should be slightly longer than the previous one. Continue alternating between shorter and longer stitches, gradually building up the area you want to fill. The key to achieving a seamless blend of colors and shading is to ensure that the stitches overlap slightly, creating a smooth transition between different shades.

As you practice the long and short stitch, you will discover that the angle and direction of your stitches play a crucial role in achieving the desired effect. Experiment with different angles and directions to create various textures and effects in your stumpwork embroidery. Remember to maintain a consistent stitch length and tension throughout your work to ensure a professional finish.

Combining Stitches for Stunning Effects of Stumpwork Embroidery: Stumpwork embroidery is a technique that involves creating three-dimensional designs on fabric using a combination of stitches and raised elements. It is a highly versatile and creative form of embroidery that allows for stunning effects and intricate details.

One of the key aspects of stumpwork embroidery is the use of different stitches to create texture and depth. By combining various stitches, such as satin stitch, long and short stitch, and French knots, embroiderers can bring their designs to life. These stitches can be used to create realistic flowers, animals, or even landscapes, adding a sense of realism and dimension to the finished piece.

In addition to stitches, stumpwork embroidery often incorporates raised elements to further enhance the three-dimensional effect. These raised elements can be created using padding techniques, such as layering felt or cotton batting underneath the fabric and stitching over it. This creates a raised surface that can be shaped and molded to add volume and dimension to the design.

Another technique commonly used in stumpwork embroidery is the use of wire to create structural elements. By inserting wire into the fabric, embroiderers can create sturdy and flexible shapes, such as leaves, wings, or even entire figures. The wire can be covered with embroidery thread or other materials to seamlessly blend it into the design.

The combination of stitches, raised elements, and wirework allows for endless possibilities in stumpwork embroidery. Embroiderers can create intricate scenes with a variety of textures and layers, resulting in stunning and eye-catching pieces of art. The level of detail and realism that can be achieved with stumpwork embroidery is truly remarkable.

While stumpwork embroidery can be a time-consuming and intricate technique, the end result is well worth the effort. The combination of stitches and raised elements creates a unique and visually striking effect that is sure to impress. Whether used to create small embellishments or large-scale designs, stumpwork embroidery offers endless possibilities for creativity and expression.

In conclusion, combining stitches for stunning effects in stumpwork embroidery allows for the creation of intricate and three-dimensional designs. By using a variety of stitches, raised elements, and wirework, embroiderers can bring their designs to life and add depth and texture to their work. The level of detail and realism that can be achieved with stumpwork embroidery is truly remarkable, making it a highly versatile and captivating form of embroidery.

Creating Realistic Florals in Stumpwork Embroidery: Creating realistic florals in stumpwork embroidery is a fascinating and intricate art form that requires skill, patience, and attention to detail. Stumpwork embroidery is a technique that involves creating three-dimensional designs by stitching layers of fabric and padding onto a base fabric. This technique allows for the creation of lifelike floral designs that appear to pop off the fabric.

To begin creating realistic florals in stumpwork embroidery, it is important to gather the necessary materials. This includes a base fabric, such as linen or cotton, embroidery threads in various colors, a needle, embroidery hoops, scissors, and a variety of fabrics for padding and shaping. Additionally, reference images of the desired flowers can be helpful for achieving a realistic look.

The first step in creating realistic florals in stumpwork embroidery is to transfer the design onto the base fabric. This can be done by tracing the design onto the fabric using a water-soluble pen or by using a transfer method such as iron-on transfers or carbon paper. Once the design is transferred, it is time to start stitching.

To create the three-dimensional effect, layers of fabric and padding are stitched onto the base fabric. This can be done using a variety of stitches, such as satin stitch, long and short stitch, and padded satin stitch. Each layer is carefully stitched and shaped to mimic the natural curves and contours of the flower petals.

When stitching the petals, it is important to pay attention to the direction of the stitches to create a realistic texture. For example, stitching in the direction of the petal's veins can add depth and dimension to the design. Additionally, using different shades of thread can help create shading and highlights, further enhancing the realistic appearance of the florals.

Once the petals are stitched and shaped, it is time to assemble the flower. This involves attaching the individual petals to the base fabric using small stitches. The petals can be arranged in a way that mimics the natural growth pattern of the flower, creating a more realistic and organic look.

To add even more realism to the design, additional elements such as leaves, stems, and buds can be stitched and attached to the base fabric. These elements can be created using the same techniques as the petals, with careful attention to detail and shading.

Creating realistic florals in stumpwork embroidery is a time-consuming process that requires patience and precision. However, the end result is a stunning and lifelike floral design that is sure to impress.

Capturing Wildlife and Insects in Thread of Stumpwork Embroidery: Stumpwork embroidery is a unique and intricate form of embroidery that involves creating three-dimensional designs on fabric. One of the fascinating aspects of stumpwork embroidery is the ability to capture the beauty and essence of wildlife and insects within the threadwork.

When it comes to capturing wildlife and insects in stumpwork embroidery, the possibilities are endless. Skilled embroiderers can recreate the delicate wings of a butterfly, the intricate patterns on a beetle's shell, or the graceful movements of a bird in flight. By using various techniques such as padding, layering, and raised stitches, these creatures can be brought to life on fabric.

To begin the process of capturing wildlife and insects in stumpwork embroidery, careful research and observation are essential. Embroiderers must study the anatomy, colors, and textures of the creatures they wish to recreate. This attention to detail ensures that the final embroidery piece is as accurate and realistic as possible.

Once the research is complete, the embroiderer can start planning the design. This involves sketching out the composition, deciding on the placement of the wildlife or insect, and determining the colors and stitches that will be used. It is important to consider the overall balance and harmony of the design, as well as the desired level of realism.

Next, the embroiderer begins the stitching process. This typically involves using a combination of traditional embroidery stitches, such as satin stitch, chain stitch, and French knots, as well as more specialized stumpwork techniques. These techniques include padding, where layers of thread or fabric are used to create a raised effect, and wired elements, where thin wires are inserted into the fabric to give structure and shape to certain parts of the design.

As the embroidery progresses, the wildlife or insect starts to take shape. The embroiderer carefully builds up the layers and textures, paying close attention to the details that make each creature unique. This can involve using different shades of thread to create depth and dimension, or adding tiny beads or sequins to mimic the shimmering scales of a fish or the iridescent wings of a dragonfly.

Finally, once the embroidery is complete, the wildlife or insect is ready to be showcased. It can be framed and displayed as a standalone piece of art, or incorporated into a larger embroidery project. The level of skill and craftsmanship required to capture wildlife and insects in stumpwork embroidery is truly remarkable, and the end result is a stunning and lifelike representation of the natural world.

Advanced Techniques: Goldwork and Silk Shading of Stumpwork Embroidery:

Stumpwork embroidery is a form of raised embroidery that creates three-dimensional designs on fabric. It involves creating padded shapes and attaching them to the fabric, resulting in a textured and sculptural effect. While stumpwork embroidery itself is a complex and intricate technique, there are advanced techniques that can take it to the next level. Two such techniques are goldwork and silk shading.

Goldwork is the art of using metallic threads, such as gold or silver, to create stunning and luxurious designs. It adds a touch of opulence and elegance to any embroidery project. In stumpwork embroidery, goldwork can be used to embellish the raised shapes and add a rich and regal touch to the overall design. Techniques such as couching, where the metallic threads are laid on the fabric and secured with smaller threads, and padding, where layers of felt or other materials are used to create a raised effect, are commonly used in goldwork. The combination of these techniques with stumpwork embroidery creates a visually striking and intricate piece of art.

Silk shading, also known as needle painting, is a technique that involves blending different shades of silk threads to create realistic and lifelike images. It is often used to depict flowers, leaves, and other natural elements in embroidery. In stumpwork embroidery, silk shading can be used to add depth and dimension to the raised shapes. By carefully selecting and blending different shades of silk threads, the embroiderer can create a realistic and vibrant effect. This technique requires a high level of skill and precision, as the embroiderer must carefully stitch each thread to create a smooth transition between colors. The result is a beautifully shaded and lifelike design that enhances the overall impact of the stumpwork embroidery.

Combining goldwork and silk shading with stumpwork embroidery allows for endless possibilities in creating intricate and visually stunning designs. The use of metallic threads adds a touch of luxury and grandeur, while silk shading brings depth and realism to the raised shapes. These advanced techniques require a high level of skill and patience, but the end result is a truly unique and breathtaking piece of art.

In conclusion, advanced techniques such as goldwork and silk shading can elevate stumpwork embroidery to new heights. The combination of metallic threads and silk shading adds richness, depth, and realism to the raised shapes, resulting in a visually striking and intricate design.

INTRODUCTION TO STUMPWORK EMBROIDERY

Embroidery is the art of decorating fabric or other materials with thread or yarn applied with a needle. Other materials such as pearls, beads, quills, and sequins may also be incorporated into embroidery. Embroidery is frequently seen on caps, hats, coats, overlays, blankets, dress shirts, jeans, gowns, stockings, and golf shirts in the present era. Embroidery can be done in a multitude of thread or yarn colors.

Among the first embroidery techniques or stitches include the chain stitch, buttonhole or blanket stitch, running stitch, satin stitch, and cross stitch.

These stitches continue to be the foundations of hand embroidery today.

CHAPTER ONE

EMBROIDER ON LEATHER

Consider how tough it is to embroider on leather. This tutorial will illustrate you how easy it is. Soon, you'll be stitching your way through all of your favorite leather things. You can also begin immediately by creating a leather card case.

As with embroidery on wood, the secret to hand stitching leather is to pre-poke the holes. After that, the embroidery is simple.

REQUIREMENTS

TOOLS / MATERIALS

Ruler

Sharp scissors

Pencil and tracing paper

Embroidery needles, large and medium sizes

Leather

Embroidery floss

Suede cording

Pattern or a easy design

Conditioner for threads (optional,

GUIDELINES

CUT THE LEATHER

Make cutting lines on the back of the leather. Begin with a 4.25" x 8.5" rectangle to create a card case large enough to hold money, gift cards, or credit or debit cards. Cut the leather using sharp scissors.

At one end, round the two corners up.

Fold the leather into the case formation, beginning with the unrounded end. It should be slightly more than 1/3 of the way in, so that the rounded end does not end up with the opposite edge when folded over.

TIP

You can purchase little pieces of leather at any craft supply stores or recycle an old leather item purchased at a second-hand store. In either scenario, you should have sufficient leather to build several card cases.

MARK THE PATTERN ON THE LEATHER

When embroidering on leather, a simple pattern such as the flower burst embroidery pattern employed here is beneficial. The fewer holes required for stitching, the simpler it is.

Trace your pattern onto tracing paper and place it on the leather where you want it. In the sample, the embroidery will be visible on the back and will wrap slightly over to the front.

Poke the tracing paper and leather at each location where the needle should pass through with a large, sharp embroidery needle.

Because the stitches are detached chain stitches, each petal shape will require a hole at the top and bottom.

TIP

While doing this and the subsequent steps, you may find it beneficial to place the leather on corrugated cardboard or cork.

INCREASE THE SIZE OF THE MARKED HOLES

When the tracing paper is removed, you should be able to see all of the other marked holes; nevertheless, they may still be tricky to deal with. Leather is frequently dense and makes it difficult to make these holes.

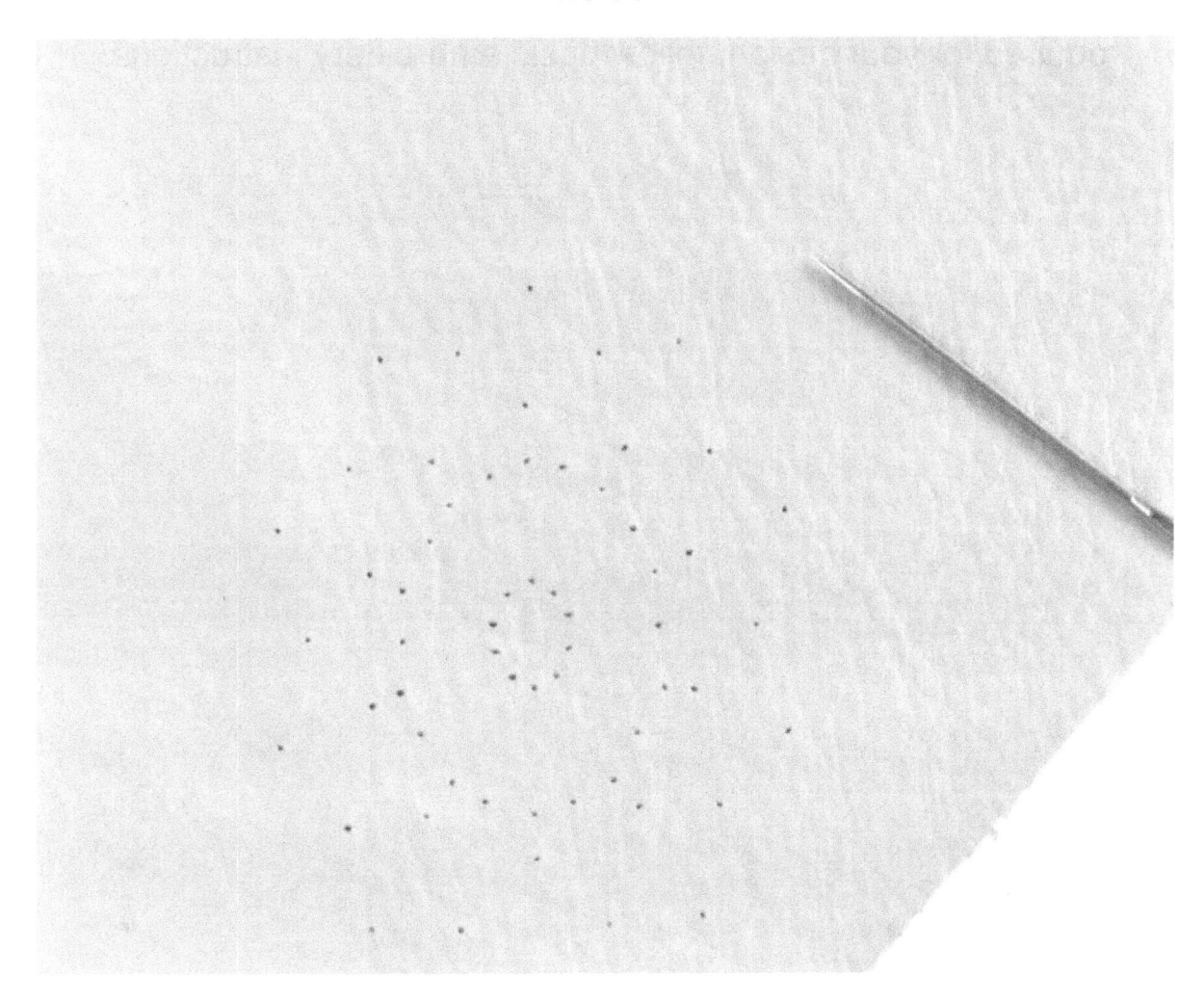

With the tracing paper set aside, widen the holes with the needle to make them easier to find while stitching.

You can use an awl to create larger holes, which is advantageous if you're embroidering with something thicker, such as Perle cotton, but a needle works just as well.

EMBROIDER THROUGH THE LEATHER

Unless you made big holes, it is better to use three strands of embroidery floss. To protect the embroidery floss as you go through the leather, run it through a thread conditioner. Once more, poke the needle through from front to back before attempting to locate the pre-punched hole from the back. Then, adhere to the stitches required for your design, follow basic embroidery instructions.

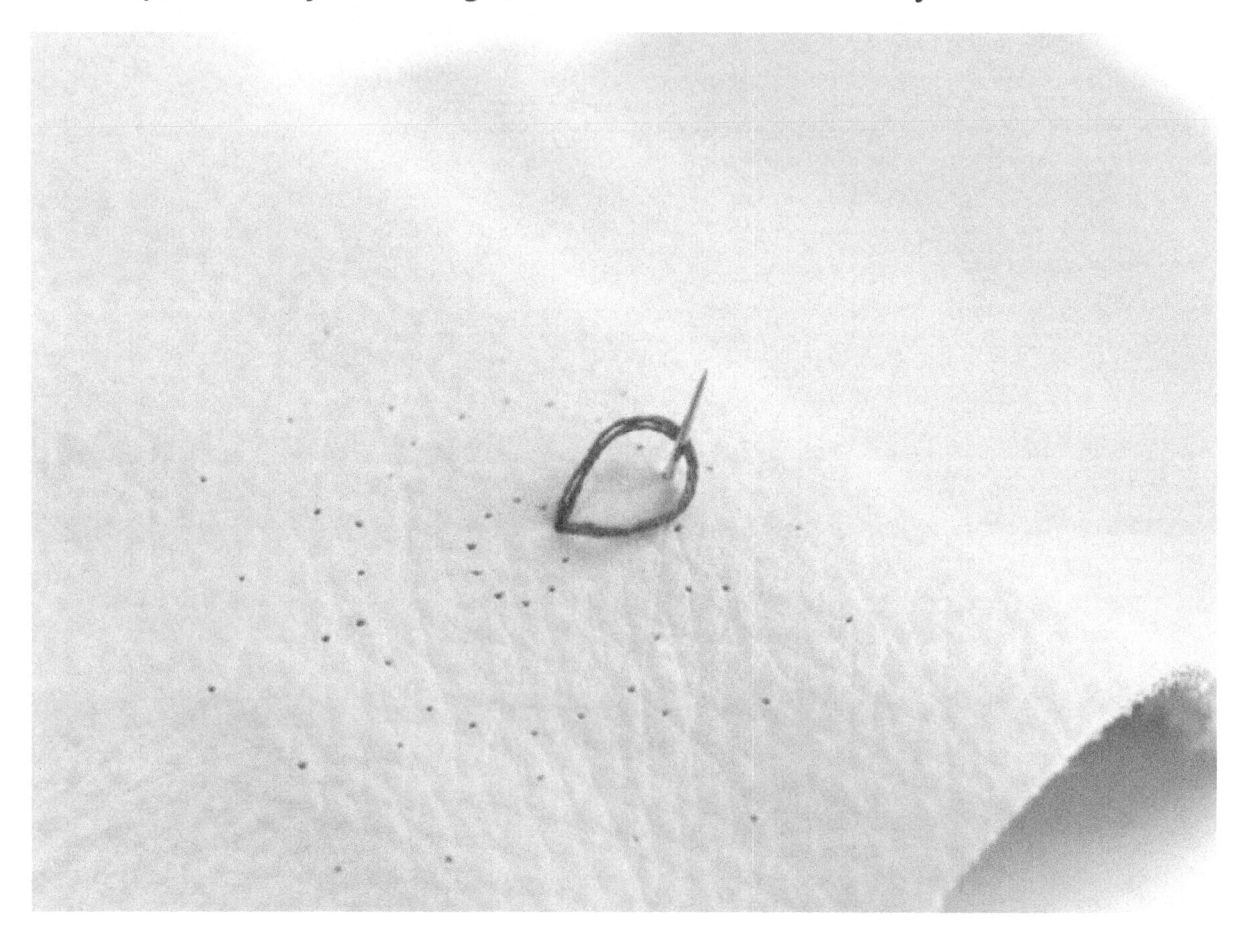

MEASURE AND MARK THE HOLES FOR THE SIDE SEAMS

Once the embroidery is complete, refold the leather into the card case shape. Using a ruler and the large needle, mark holes a quarter inch from the edge and from each other.

This should be repeated on the back of the card case and then on the opposite edge, both front and back.

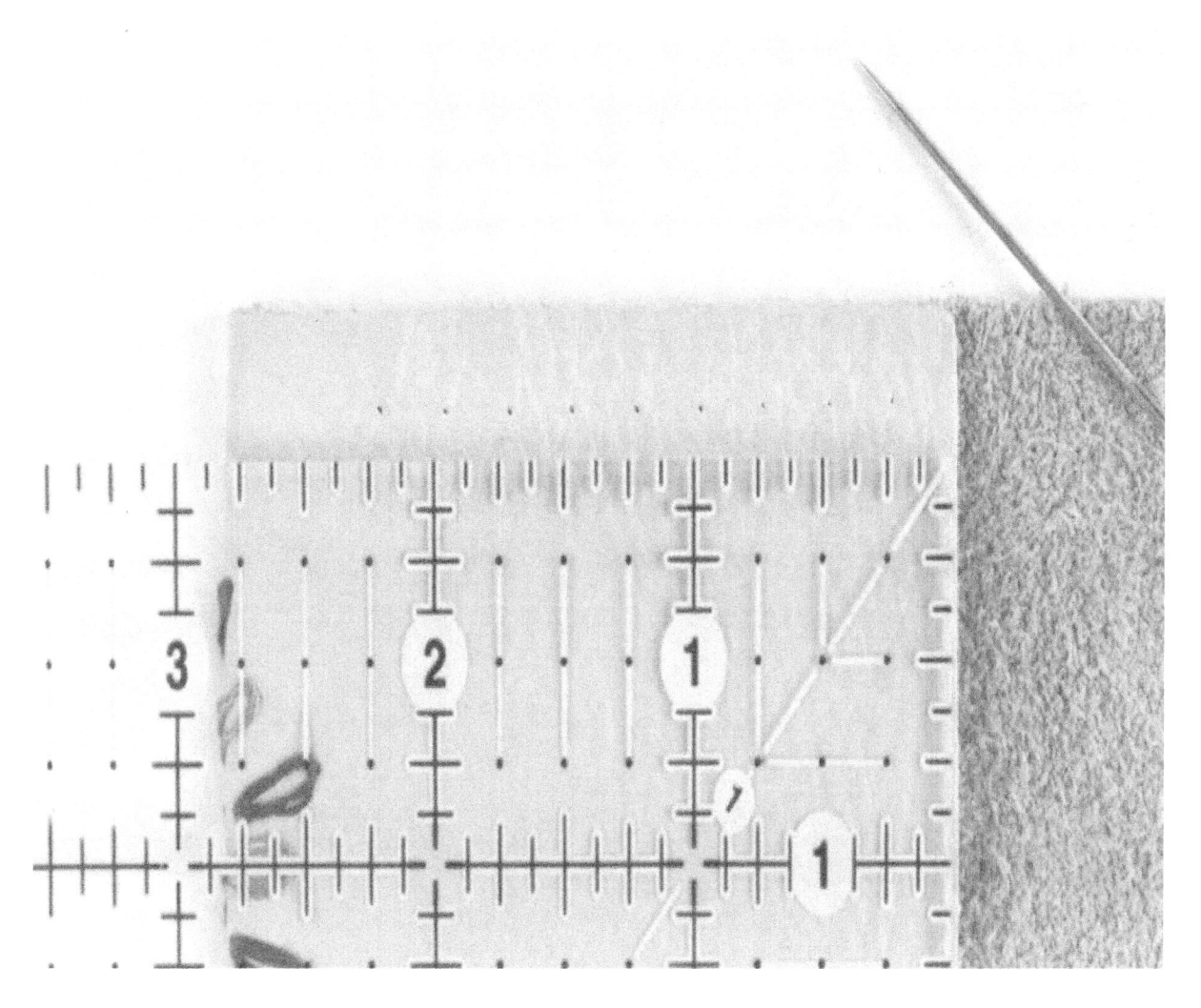

SEW THE SIDES OF THE CARD CASE TOGETHER

Stitch the card case's sides together using a double running stitch through the marked holes. Begin with the first line of running stitch at the top of the opening and work your way down the line, filling in the gaps. Additionally, it is beneficial to use a thread conditioner for this step.

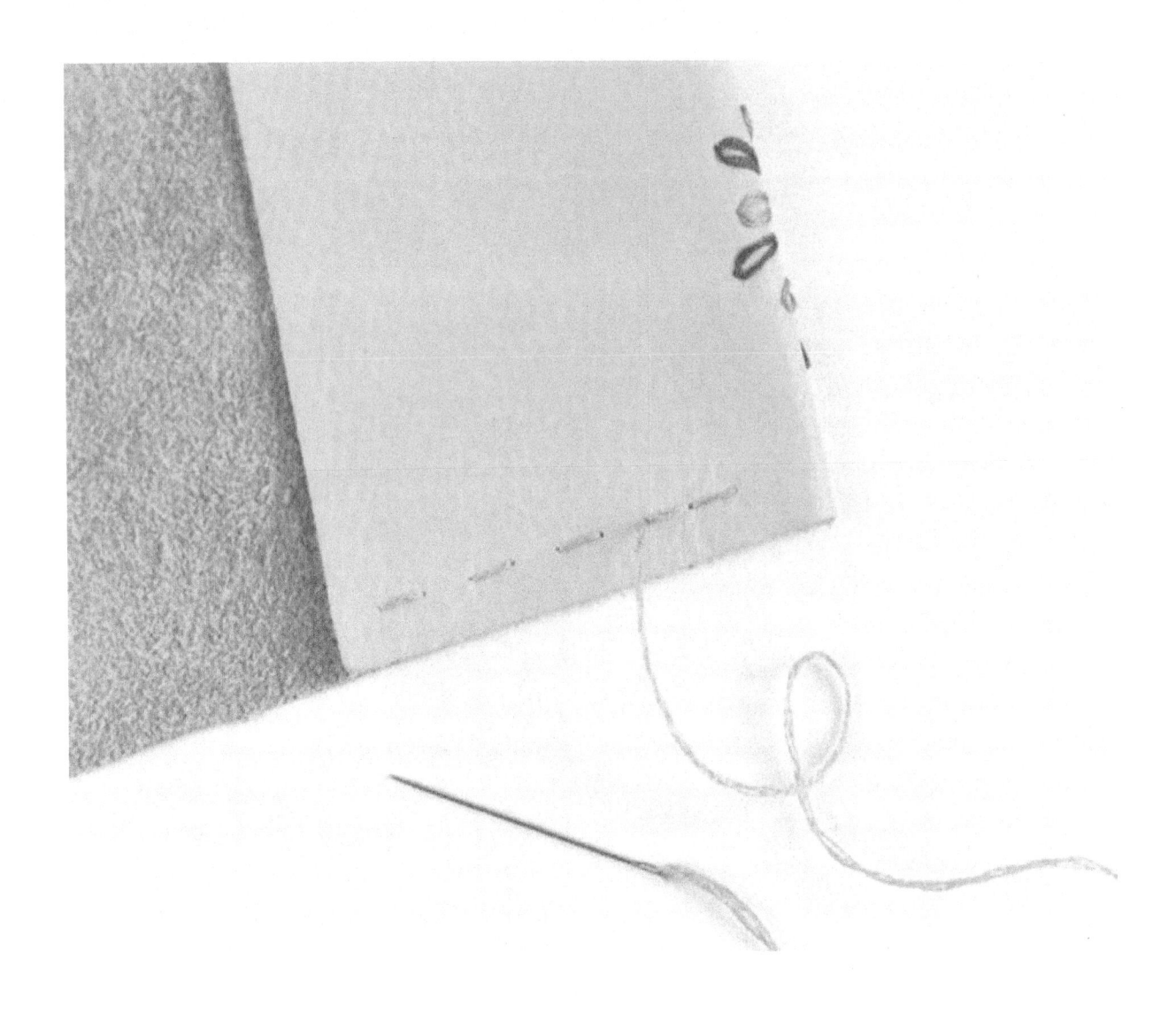

ATTACH THE CORD TO THE FLAP

Make two small slits in the flap of the card case, parallel to the edge and centered.

Cut a 24-inch length of suede cord and tie one end with a doubled knot. Slide the other end through the flap's slits and tie a doubled knot on the cord's other end.

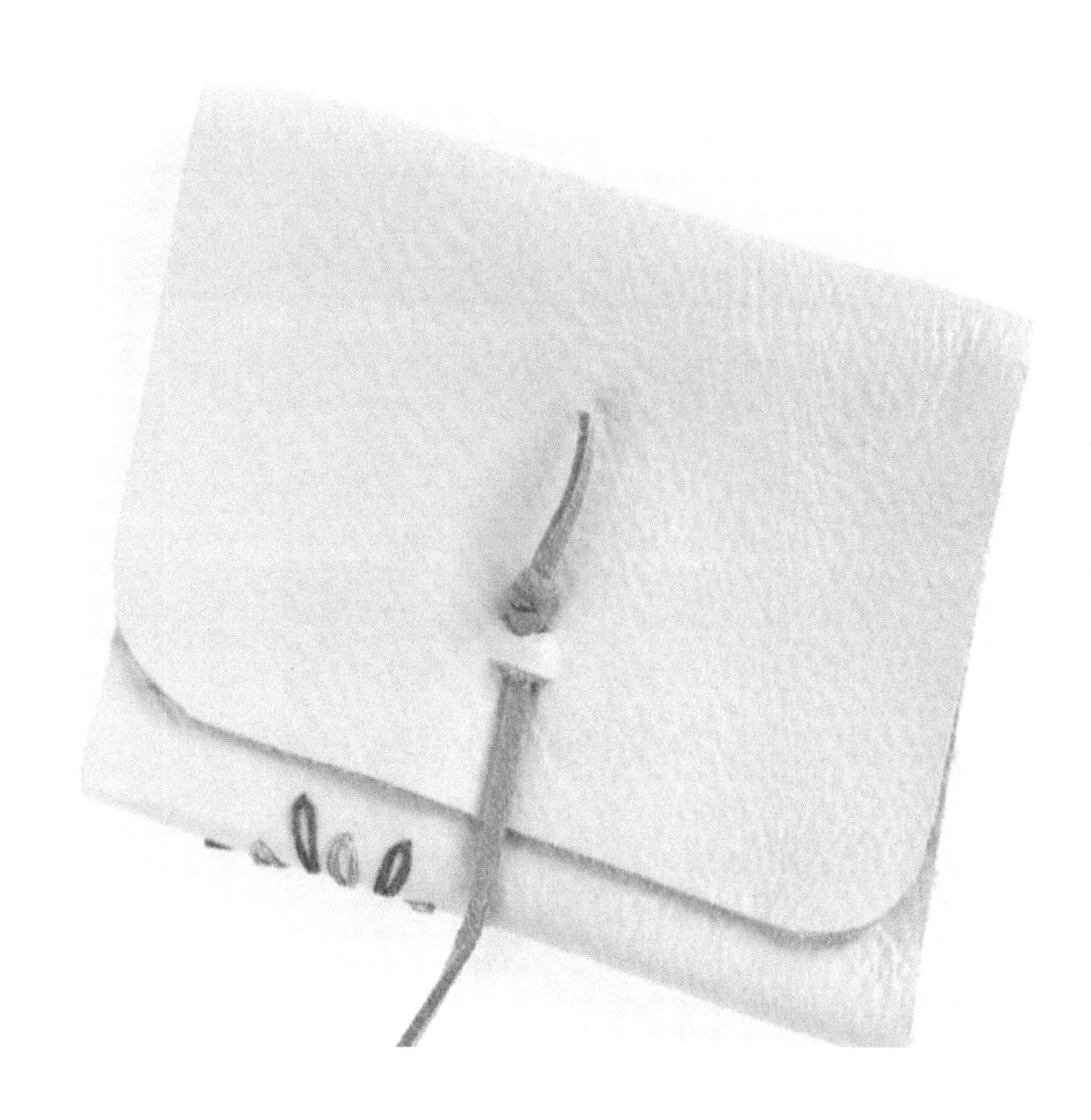

WRAP THE CORD AROUND THE CASE TO HOLD IT CLOSE

Wrap the cable multiple times around the card case's flap to secure it. Tuck the knotted end beneath the wrapping to secure it.

YOUR CARD IS READY

This case is very useful in holding a little amount of money and a few cards. Since its leather, it will even stretch a bit over time if you want to use it to hold other things. It's also an ideal way to present gift cards with a bit of traditional style.

CHAPTER TWO
DIY EMBROIDERED BARGELLO

With only one easy stitch to master, Bargello is an excellent beginner needlepoint technique for creating modern embroidery designs that are enjoyable to stitch! Simple stitches are transformed into geometric designs and whimsical patterns.

You don't need a lot of materials and what you do need is relatively cheap, but if you want to get started without having to worry about finding the right items, Hello Bargello is an excellent source for kits. And, while this kind of needlework dates all the way back to the 17th century, there are numerous contemporary books and patterns to draw inspiration from. Additionally, you can create your own!

BRIEF HISTORY ABOUT BARGELLO

Bargello (uttered bar-jello) is a type of needlepoint or embroidered using counted threads. It is also known as Florentine work or flame stitch embroidery, which is derived from a design on some chairs in Florence's Bargello Palace that feature a "flame design." Additionally, this motif has inspired a quilt pattern.

Bargello embroidery patterns employ lengthy stitches on a grid to produce geometric shapes with the appearance of movement or optical illusions. Of course, numerous designs deviate from this basic aesthetic.

REQUIREMENTS

TOOLS / MATERIALS

18 plastic canvas needle

Scissors

10 mesh plastic canvas

Tapestry wool

GUIDELINES

MATERIALS AND PATTERNS

Due to the fact that Bargello is a type of counted thread embroidery, the patterns are presented on a grid or chart. Always keep an eye on the number of holes skipped to produce a stitch as you work through a design.

There are numerous materials available for Bargello, but the most frequently used are plastic canvas or needlepoint canvas, as well as tapestry or Persian wool. Select a canvas size and tapestry yarn that is both large enough to cover the canvas. Ten-mesh plastic canvas and tapestry wool are excellent places to begin since they provide ample structure and the yarn is durable.

PREPARE TO STITCH

Trim the size of your canvas as desired. Trim plastic canvas to the precise size required, paying attention to the smoothness of the edges. Trim the needlepoint canvas to leave an inch or so extra on all sides, and then tape the raw edges with masking tape.

When working with large designs, it can be beneficial to begin in the middle. It's best to begin near the top, at the edge on this small piece. Each stitch in Bargello is worked from bottom to top (or top to bottom, although for the purposes of this tutorial, we're working bottom to top), always following the same pattern.

To begin, start at one end of the stitch line specified on the pattern chart. Leave a short tail on the canvas's back. This will be secured with the first stitches.

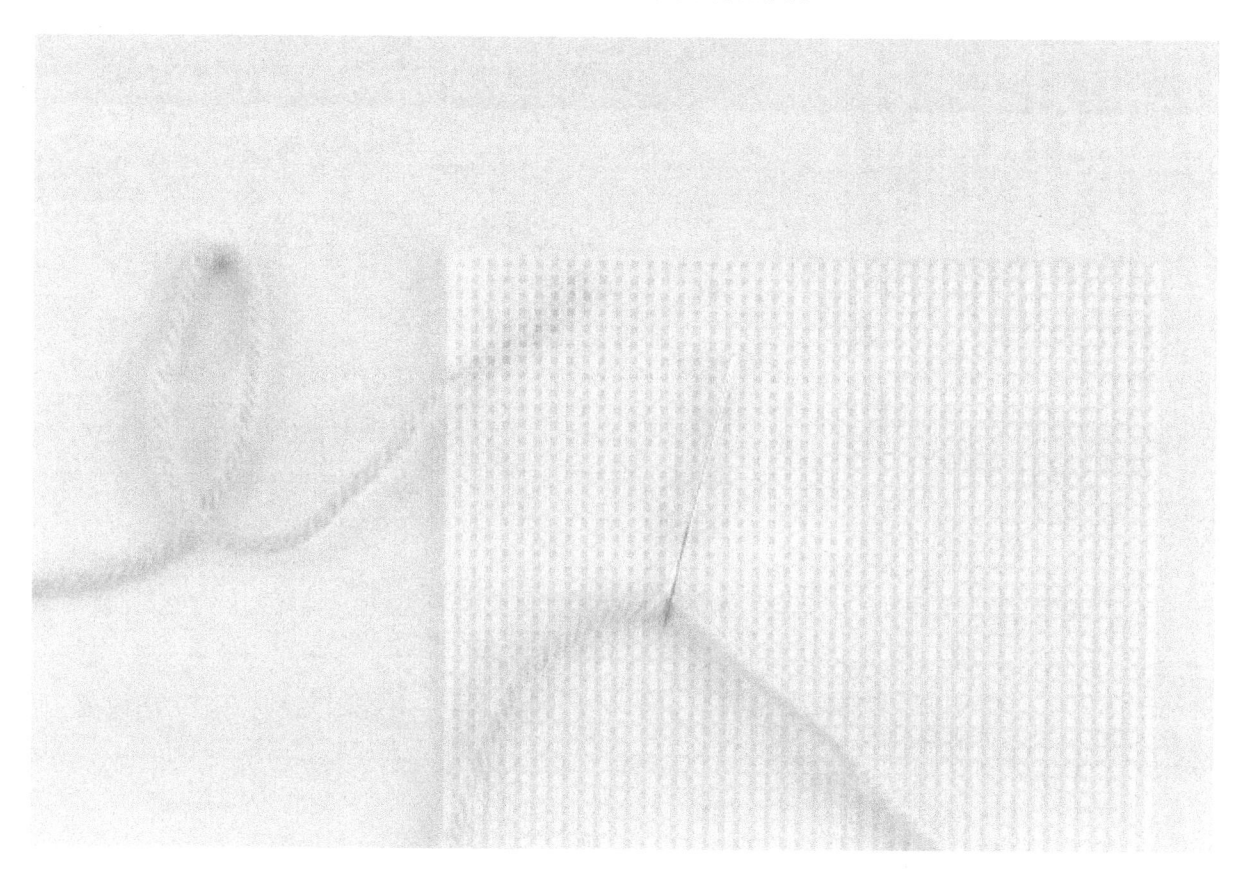

MAKE YOUR FIRST BARGELLO STITCHES

Count the number of holes on the pattern that need to be skipped, thereafter skip those and return to the bottom of the canvas.

At the bottom of the next stitch, pass through the canvas and then return to the top of the stitch.

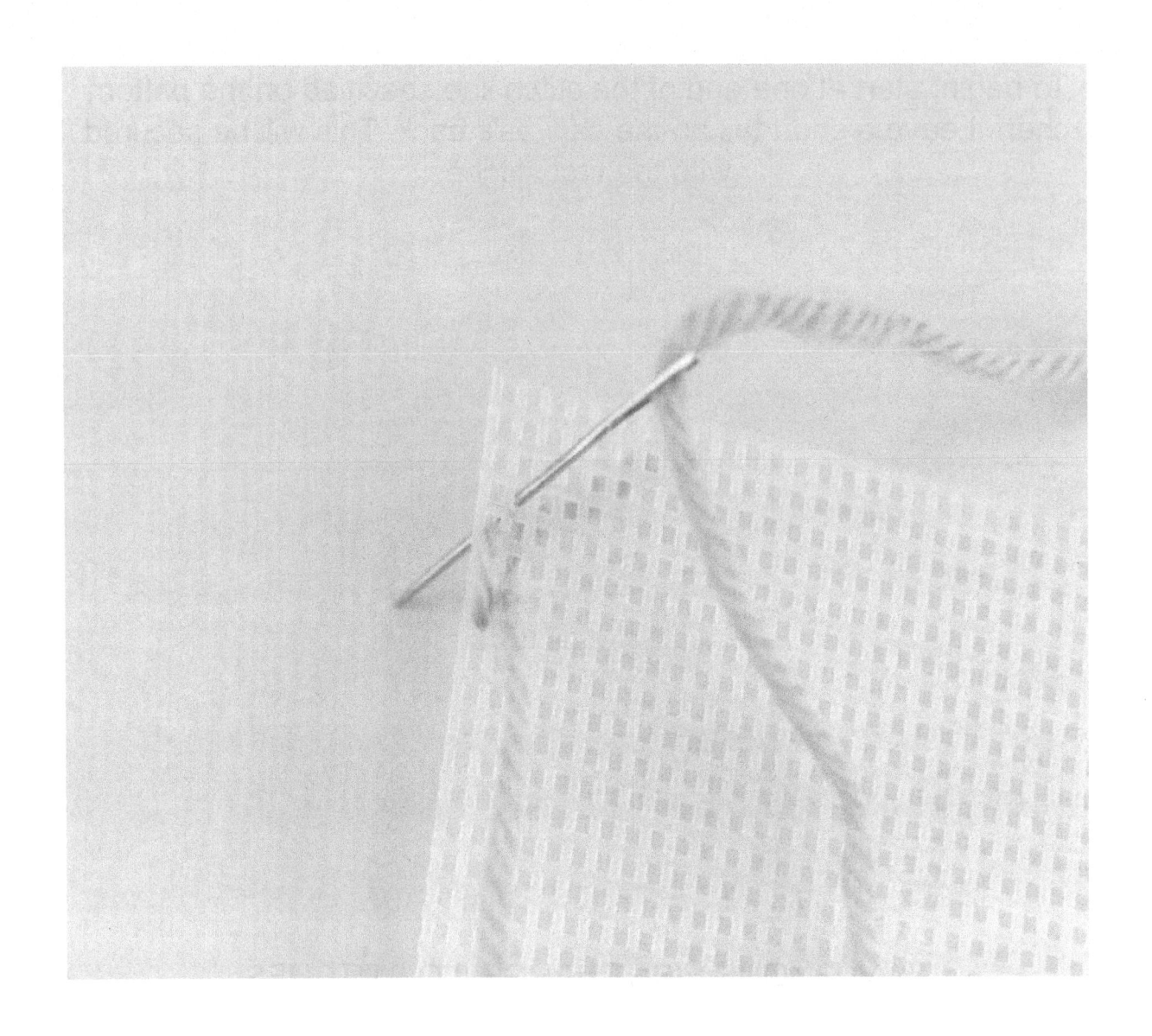

As you work, check that the stitches completely cover the beginning tail on the back of the canvas.

WORK THE STAGGERED STITCHES AND SECURE THE END

Continuing the pattern across the row, add additional stitches. Even though it appears to make more sense to work the stitches from top to bottom at times (as occurs when a line slopes downward), always work a row of stitches consistently.

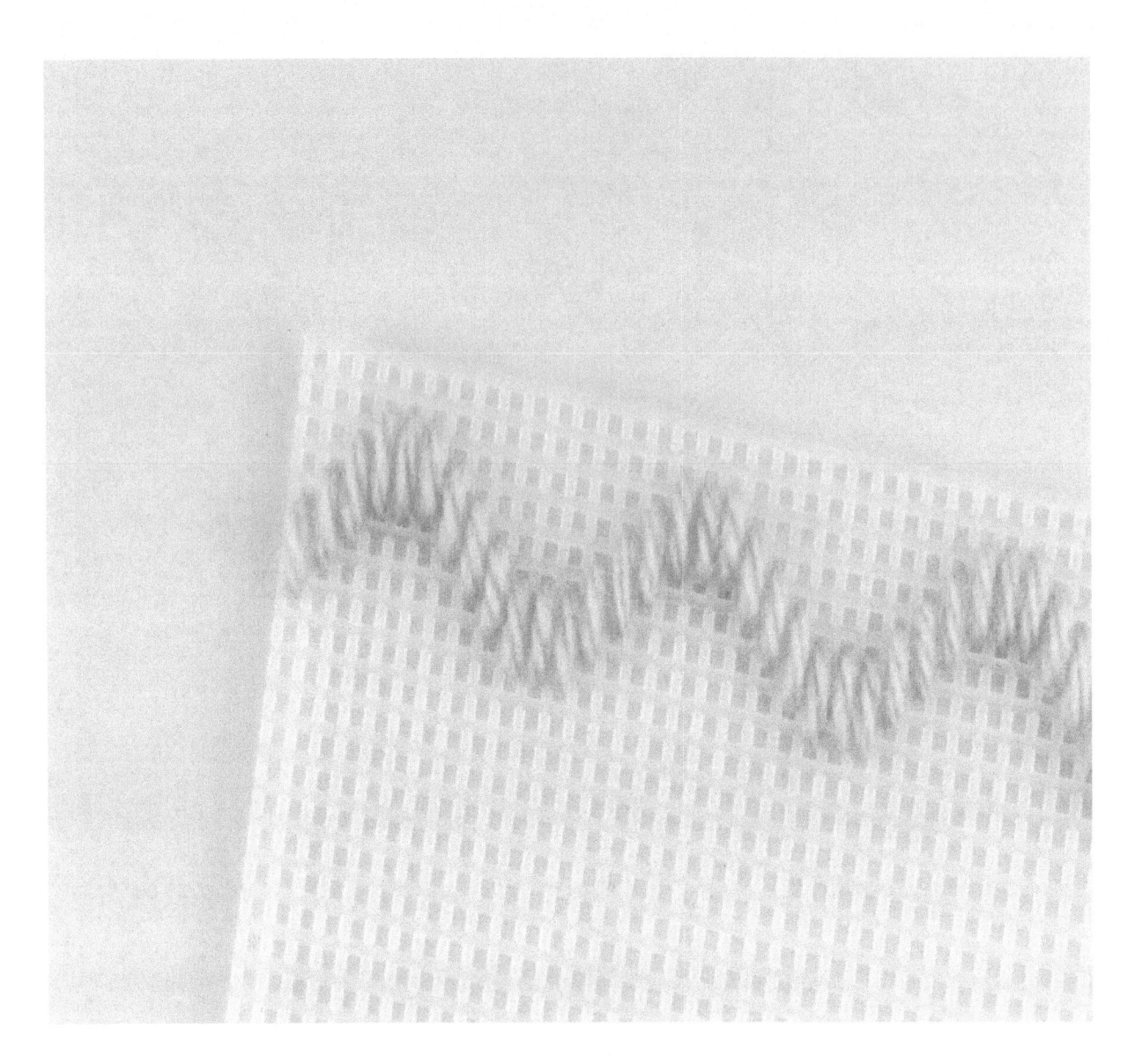

When the length of yarn runs out, secure it by sliding it through the back of the previously completed stitches.

Continue to slide the tail through the matching yarn wherever possible to prevent any colors from showing through on the front.

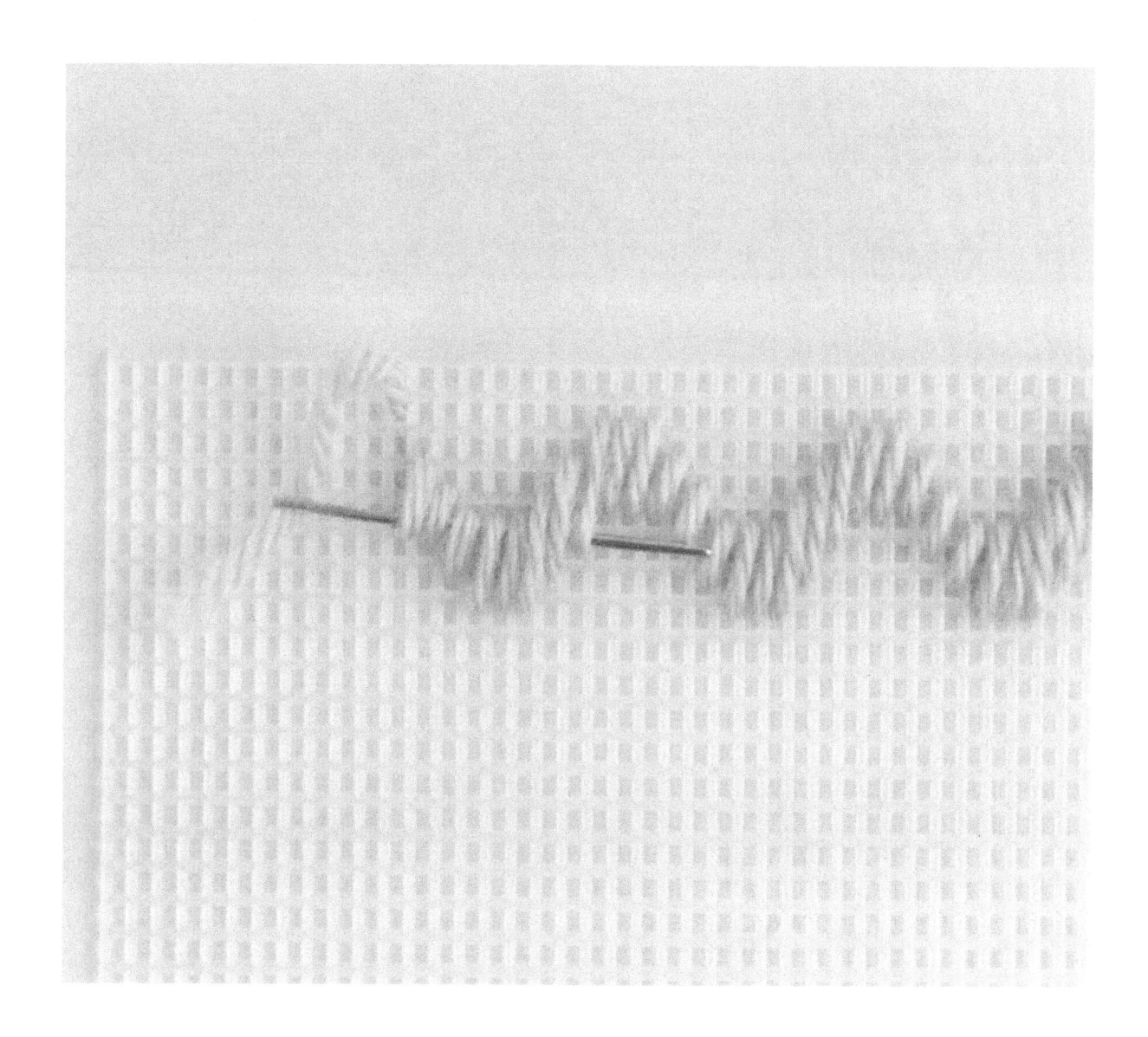

INCREASE THE STITCHES BY ADDING MORE ROWS

Stitch the following row. In some patterns, like as this one, each row of color uses stitches of the same length, but this is not always the case, so pay close attention to those indications!

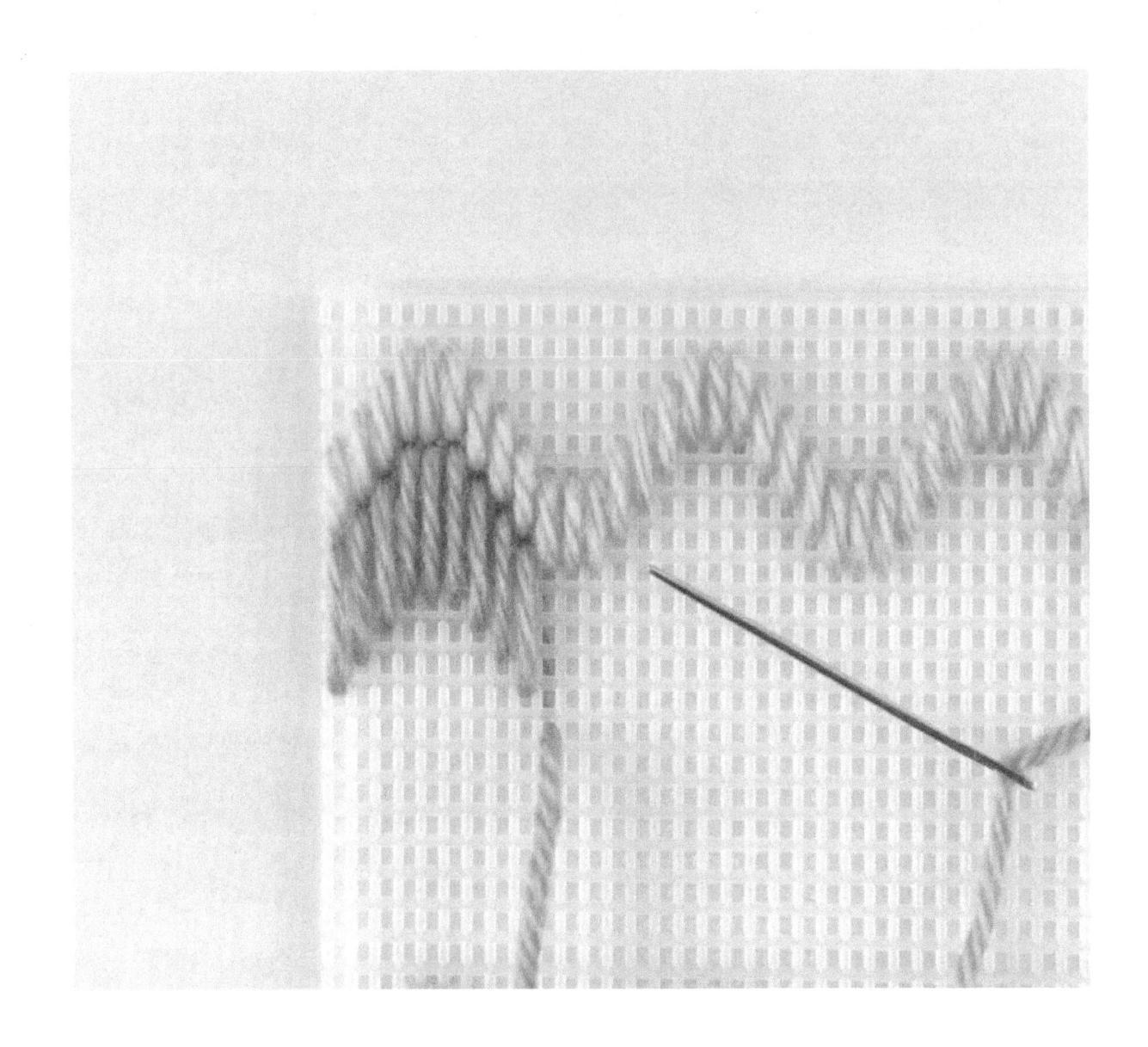

To completely fill in the shape of this (and many other) designs, you'll need some extremely little stitches. They do not display much, but they are vital, so do not overlook them!

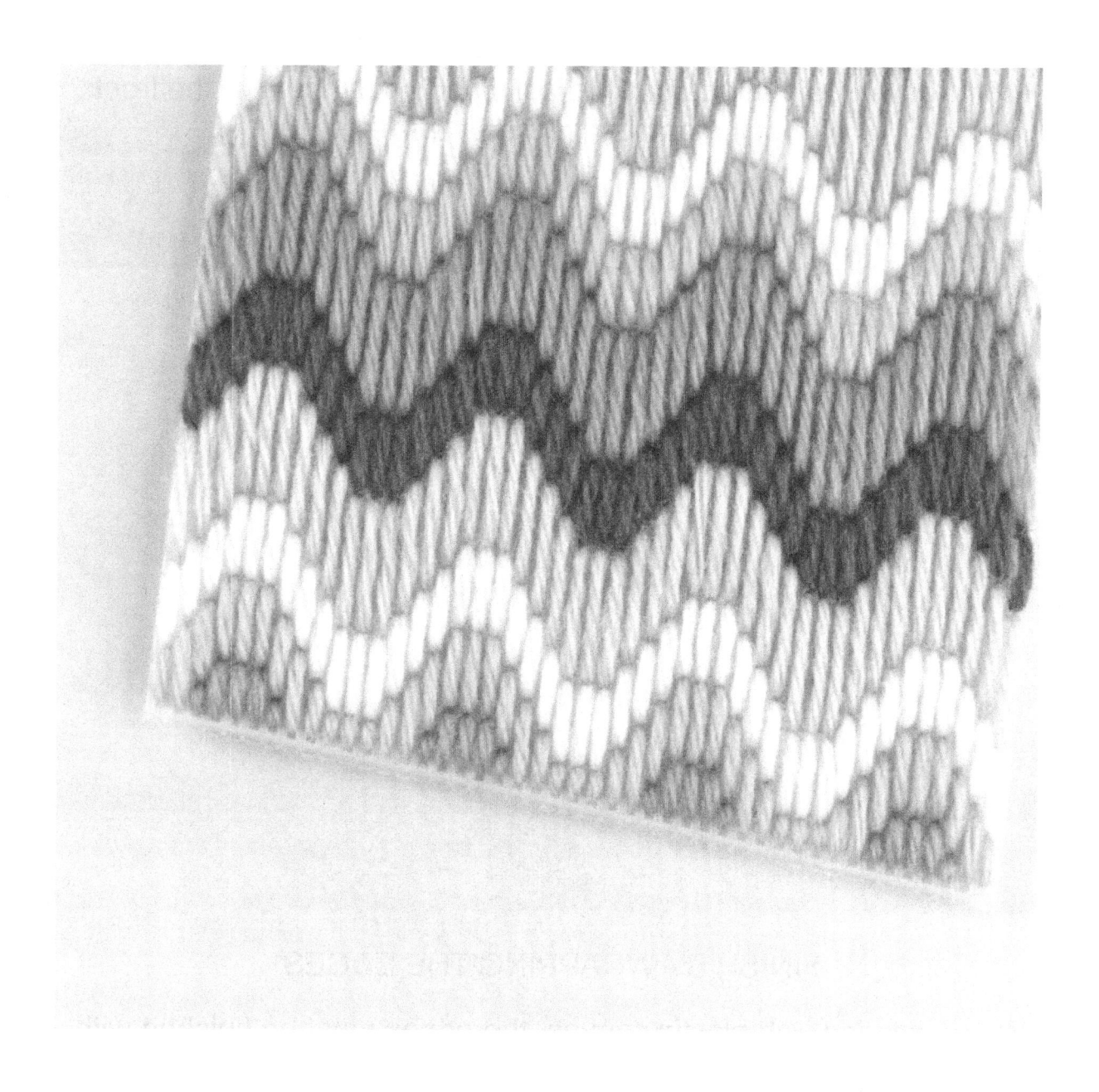

KEEP THE BACK EVEN

The back of Bargello needlework varies in appearance based on the stitch length and the amount of stepping up and down between the stitches, but it is normally quite even. There may be minor gaps where you ended of a length of yarn or where the stitches stepped up or down, but the smooth and solid parts contribute to the front being smooth and solid as well.

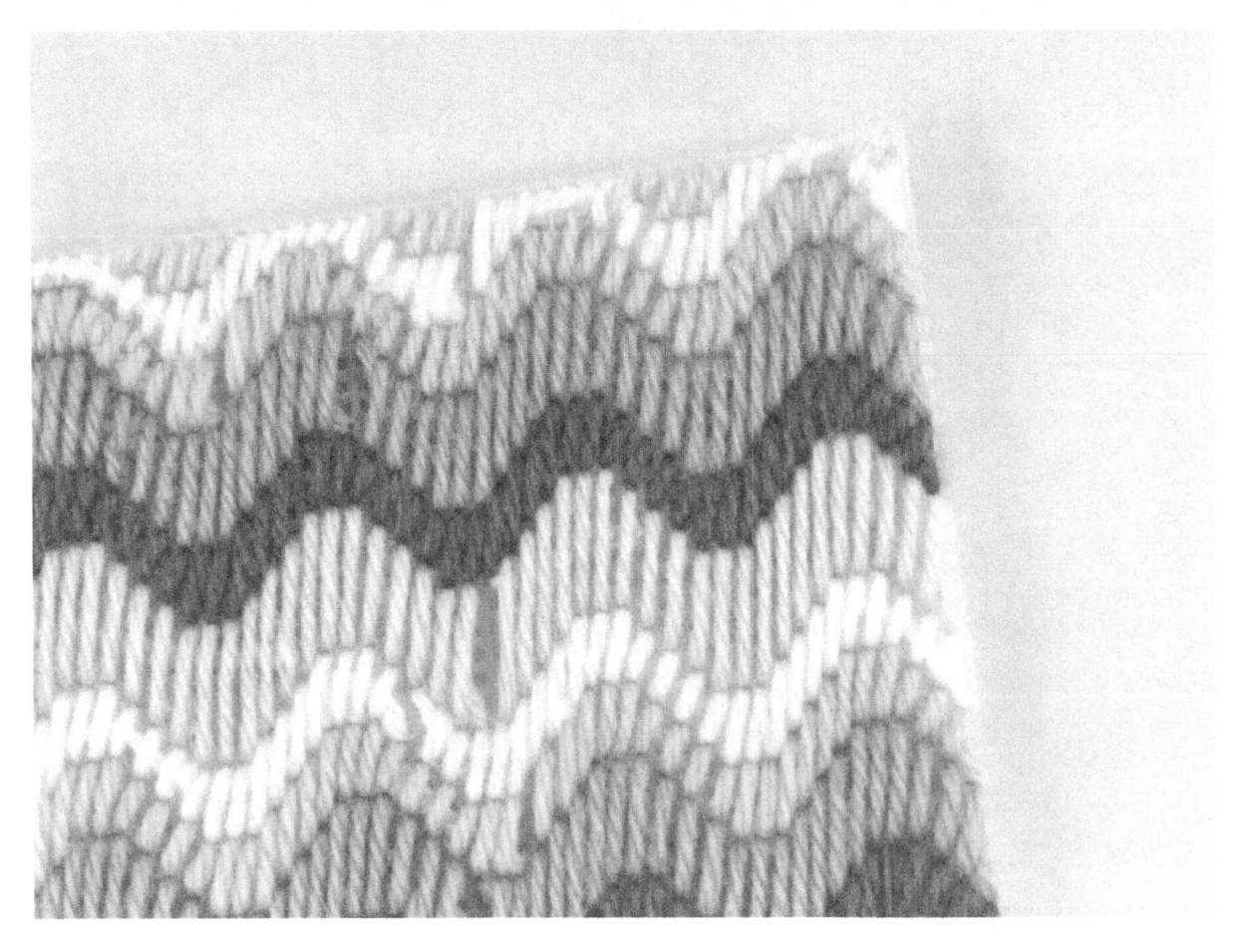

FINISH BY WRAPPING THE EDGES

When working with plastic canvas, the edges must be finished with whip stitch (similar to an overcast stitch).

Begin by stitching over the yarn tail around the edge of the plastic canvas. Always bring the tapestry wool through the back from the back.

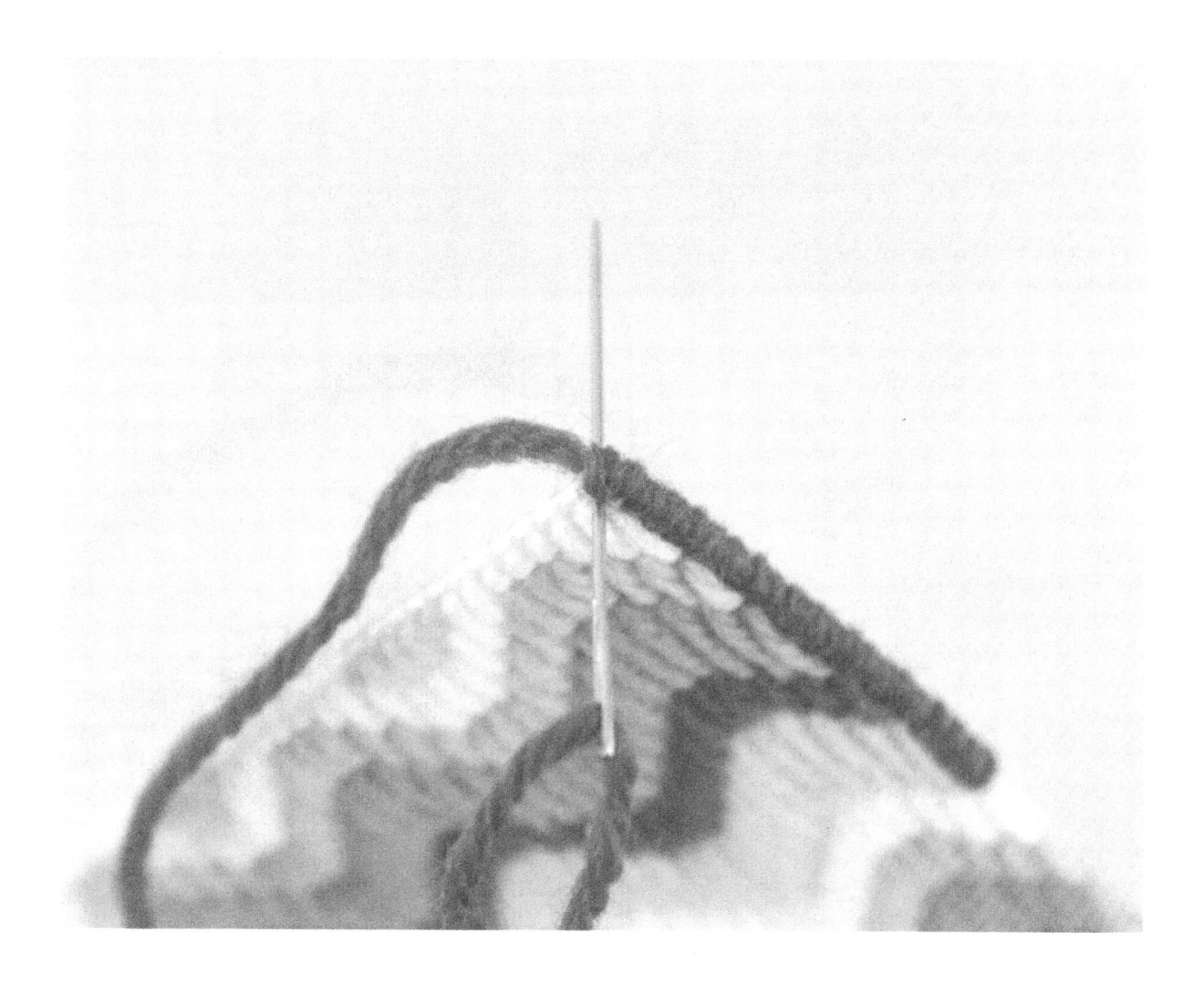

Stitch through the corner hole three times at the corners: one for the first edge, one to cover the corner's point, and one for the second edge. This completely encloses the corner, ensuring that no visible plastic is visible.

To complete the tapestry wool, carefully thread the needle through the back of previously produced whip stitches. It's acceptable to capture only a portion of the yarn as long as you secure it without interrupting the stitches.

When working on needlepoint canvas, do the project as you would with any other type of needlepoint or as specified in the project's instructions.

Make a coaster out of your completed Bargello piece or add a hanging to display it on your wall! This is only the beginning of how you can use this embroidery technique to create stunning and contemporary designs. You may create virtually any form of plastic canvas item (think planters, bags, and tissue box covers), as well as a variety of needlepoint projects such as ornaments, belts, and pillows!

Very beautiful as table cloth for your dining table.

CHAPTER THREE
DIY EMBROIDERED SWEATER

Are you a sucker for curling up in a warm sweater on a crisp, cool day? Embroider the collar of your favorite pullover with your enthusiasm for sweater weather! A touch of hand-stitching elevates a ready-made or handcrafted sweater to new heights.

Because sweaters stretch, precise stitching is required. It is recommended that you work without an embroidery hoop. However, the procedure is simple when you use tracing paper to mark your pattern. Not only does the paper indicate which stitches to use, but it also serves as a stabilizer for your needlework.

TIP

When shopping for a sweater, aim for one with a reasonably smooth fabric. While chunky knits work, they are more challenging to embroider uniformly.

WHAT YOU WILL REQUIRE

EQUIPMENT / MATERIALS

Pencil

Scissors

Needle

Sweater

Floss for embroidery

Paper for tracing

Thread

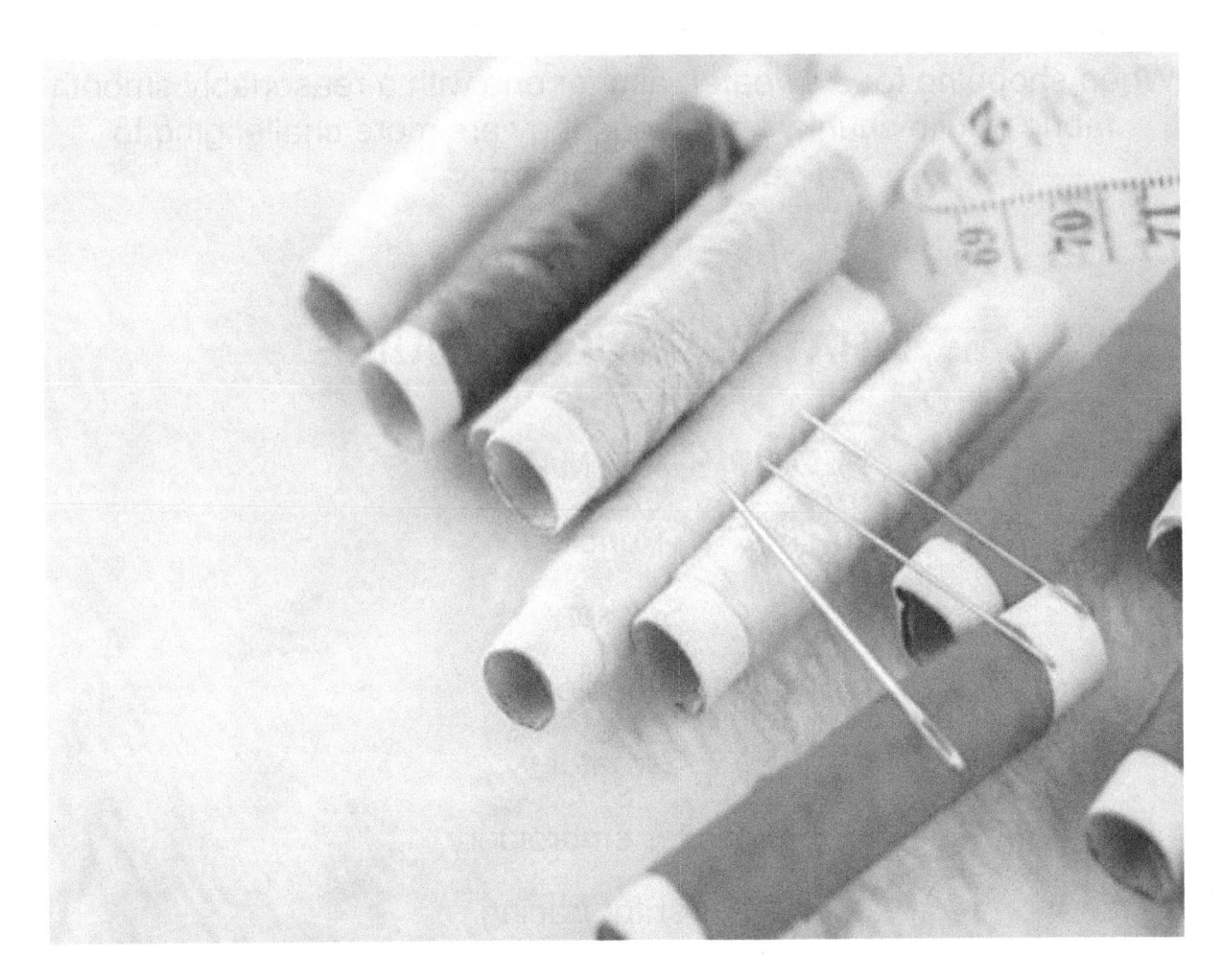

GUIDELINES FOR THE SWEATER

PRINT AND DOWNLOAD THE PATTERN

The Sweater Weather pattern is available for download from the web, as many others. Print the pattern in the size that you wish; the pattern page provides three variations, each with a slightly different curve. Comparing the patterns to the neckline of your sweater can help you determine which one works best.

Sweater Weather

Sweater Weather

Sweater Weather

TIP

If you're not comfortable using the phrase "sweater weather," you can write anything in your own handwriting or print it out in a basic font.

TRACE THE PATTERN

Trace the pattern onto tracing paper with an ordinary pencil. Cut loosely around the pattern, leaving a 1/2-inch border around the words.

BASTE THE PATTERN TO THE SWEATER

Baste the tracing paper pattern down the neckline of the sweater using ordinary thread and long-running stitches. As you attach the paper, check to ensure that the design is aligned with the neckline. If the stitching is wrong now, the embroidery will be crooked as well.

EMBROIDER THE DESIGN

Begin your embroidery with an away knot, which will temporarily hold the end of the embroidery floss. A standard knot at the thread's end will draw the thread through the sweater and is therefore insecure.

Using your preferred basic stitch, embroider the design. The sample utilizes three strands and reverses chain stitch, but you can substitute a backstitch for the reverse chain stitch.

TIP

If you wish to make some of the lines thicker than others, you can add a second line of stitching directly next to the first, but this is best done after removing the paper in the following step.

When stopping a thread and beginning a new one, secure the ends behind the previous stitches. After you've completed all of the embroidery, carefully clip the away knot. Weave the end of the loose thread through the back of the completed stitches.

REMOVE THE PAPER TEMPLATE

Remove the basting stitches from the tracing paper to complete your embroidered sweater. Following that, carefully take away the paper.

Tear along the stitching's margins, but avoid tugging on the stitches excessively. Occasionally, paper fragments become lodged beneath the stitching. If this occurs, gently remove the pieces with a needle and/or tweezers.

CHAPTER FOUR

DIY SWEDISH HUCK EMBROIDERY

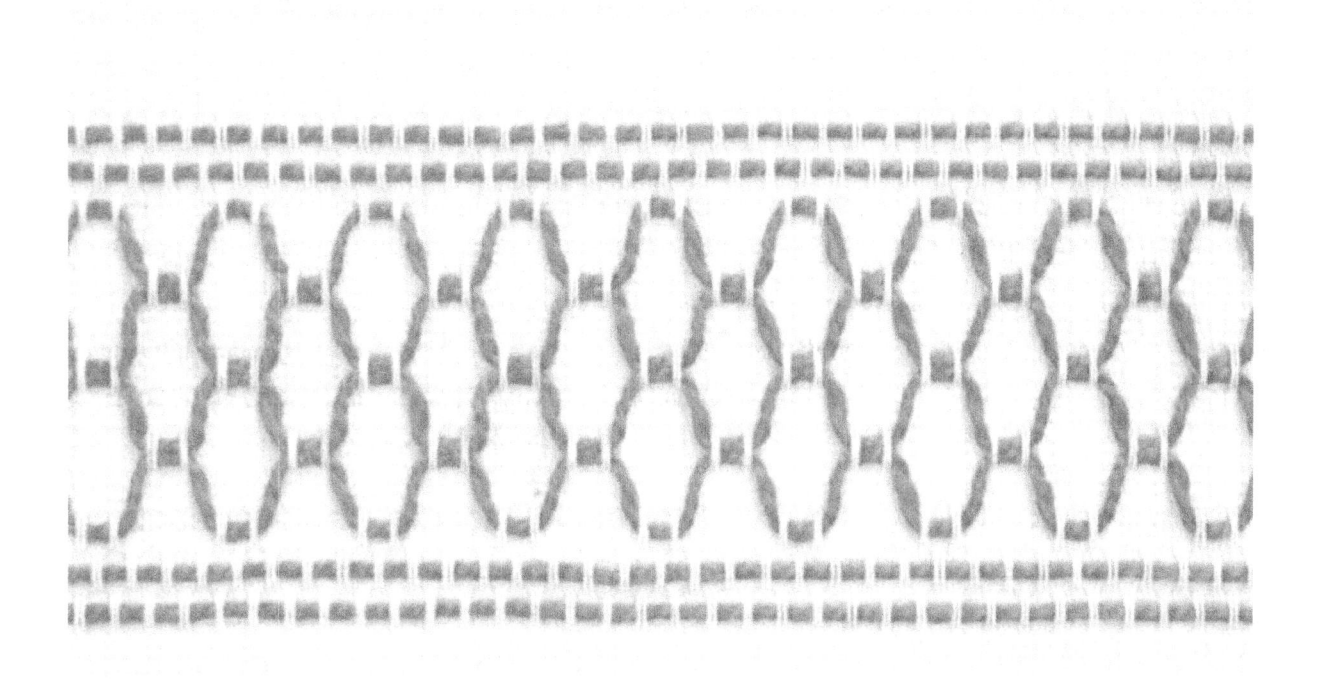

Huck embroidery, also known as huck weaving or Swedish weaving, is a type of embroidery that combines surface embroidery and weaving techniques. It gets its name from the huck cloth that is the most frequently used material for this style, and as the alternate name implies, huck needlework originated in Sweden. It is frequently found on tablecloths and towels.

Huck embroidery patterns range widely in complexity, from simple bands to words or motifs to intricate all-over designs. But, just like with counted cross-stitch, blackwork, and other kinds of counted thread embroidery, the method is just simple if you learn to follow a pattern or chart.

Additionally, this type of embroidery is extremely quick to do, making it an excellent choice for creating tiny gifts for friends and family.

SUPPLIES FOR HUCK EMBROIDERY

FABRIC

Due to the way huck embroidery weaves the thread through the fabric; specific fabric intended for this purpose is required. Fabrics appropriate for huck weaving frequently feature a layer of "floating" warp or weft threads, which allows you to stitch solely under these threads. As a result, the embroidery is fully on the fabric's surface and never penetrates the fabric's back.

Numerous fabrics are suitable for huck stitching, however each performs slightly differently and outcomes may vary. If you're following a pattern, take note of the recommended or needed fabric. A self-fringing edge can also be added to the majority of these textiles.

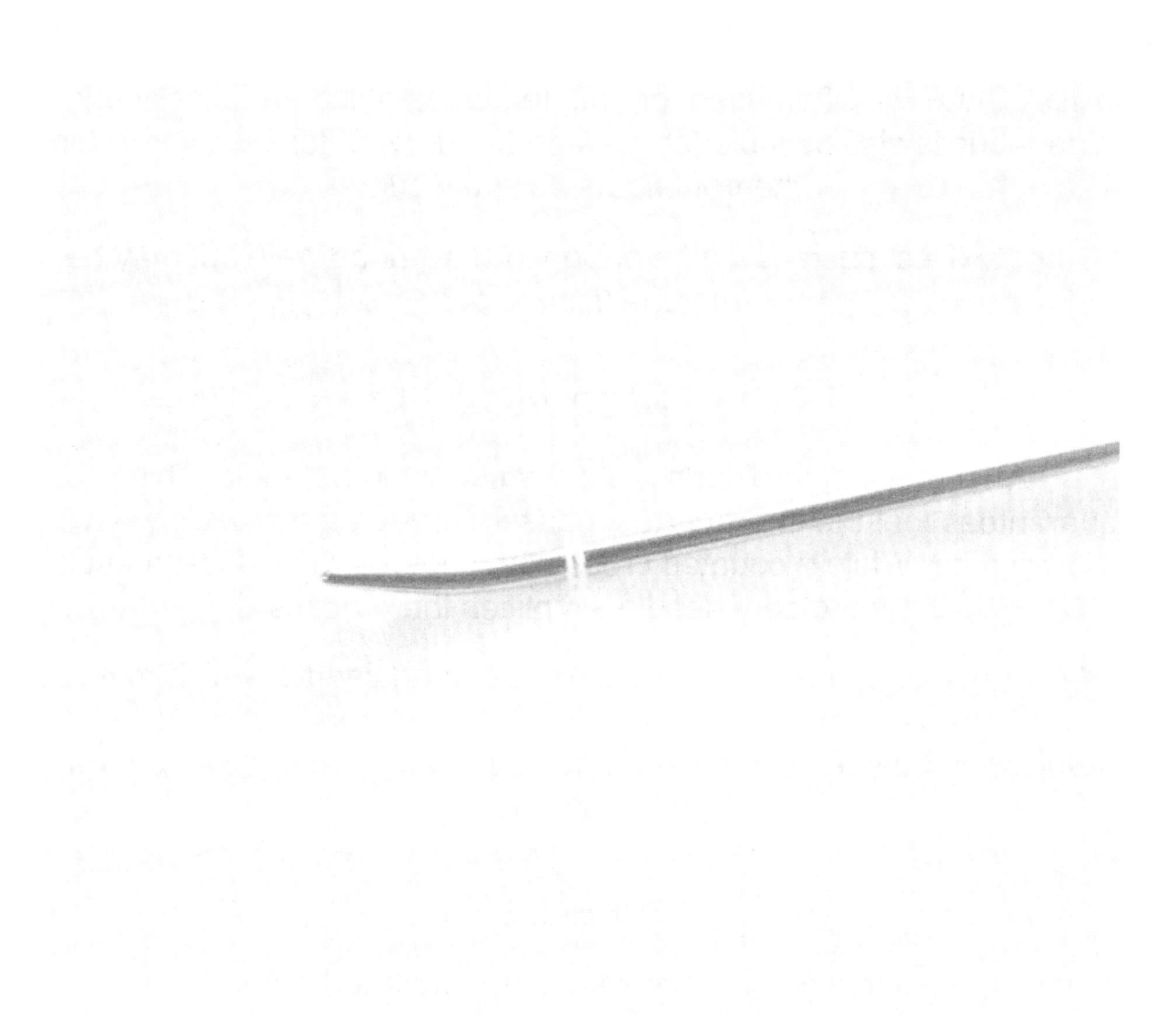

HUCK FABRIC - This is the most frequently used fabric for huck embroidery, and it is really simple to work with. Huck fabric is composed entirely of vertical floats through which you may thread your needle. Additionally, this material is frequently available as toweling, with two sides completed at a width that is ideal for manufacturing tea towels, or you can look for finished huck towels.

MONK'S CLOTH – Select monk's cloth for a thicker fabric. This fabric has both horizontal and vertical floats and should always be pre-washed prior to use. Monk's cloth is widely used to make Afghans and other large items with huck needlework.

AIDA CLOTH - Often used for counted cross-stitch and blackwork, Aida fabric is also suitable for huck embroidery. Stitch solely through the front floats as you work.

Other textiles, such as waffle or popcorn, work as well, but may be more difficult to get.

NEEDLES

When huck embroidering, always use a blunt needle. This guarantees that the thread is just passed through the fabric's weave, not pierced. While a counted cross-stitch needle will suffice, a huck embroidery needle simplifies the process.

Huck embroidery needles have a blunt and angled tip, which makes scooping the needle beneath the floating threads effortless. Additionally, these needles are longer, allowing you to cover a large area in one pass.

THREADS

Huck embroidery can be done with either stranded embroidery floss or Perle cotton. Although the examples in this article all uses Perle cotton size 5, other sizes and varieties are acceptable. Indeed, any thread that is colorfast and pulls smoothly through the floats will work.

Nordic Needle is a wonderful source for supplies and kits if you wish to order everything at once.

GUIDELINES

GETTING STARTED WITH HUCK EMBROIDERY AND STITCHING IT

LENGTH OF THREAD

It is recommended that thread lengths not exceed 18 inches be used for standard embroidery. You'll frequently need significantly longer lengths of thread for huck stitching. The pattern will specify the length of each piece based on the type of stitch used in a row.

If a pattern specifies a 2T thread, for example, you should cut a piece twice the width of the fabric being stitched.

To help prevent tangling on longer pieces, you may want to use thread conditioner.

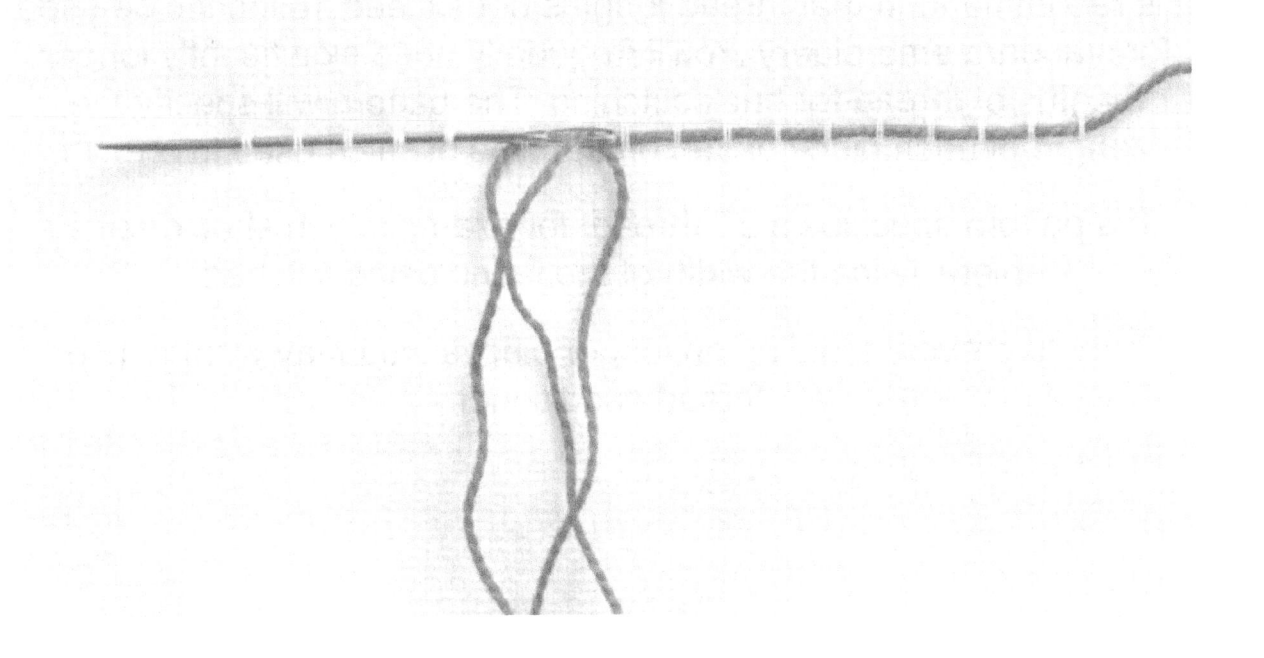

WHERE TO START

When performing huck embroidery, it is unnecessary to work in a hoop. Indeed, without a hoop, it is much easier to move the fabric more freely when the needle passes beneath the floats.

Numerous huck patterns include a design that should be centered horizontally on whatever you're stitching. As a result, it is recommended to begin in the middle and proceed to the left and right.

Using a crease or a safety pin, determine the fabric's center. Thread your needle and insert it beneath the first pair of floats that you're stitching. Draw the thread through to the center of the fabric, with the centre of the thread at the middle of the fabric.

Stitch the design in one direction first, then remove the needle, thread the opposite side of the thread, and continue stitching in the opposite direction. This is much easier to perform if you flip your work around so that one side is facing in the opposite direction.

You can work from one side to the other for patterns that do not require centering.

FINISHING HUCK EMBROIDERY THREAD ENDS

No knots are used in huck embroidery. When you approach the end of the stitching area, pull the needle back through the same floats, skipping the previous set. Stitch at least five times or more, depending on whether the item will be laundered.

If you're starting on one side and working your way around the design, follow the same procedure. Simply take at least five stitches in the other way from the direction in which you will be working and then double back as you work the designs.

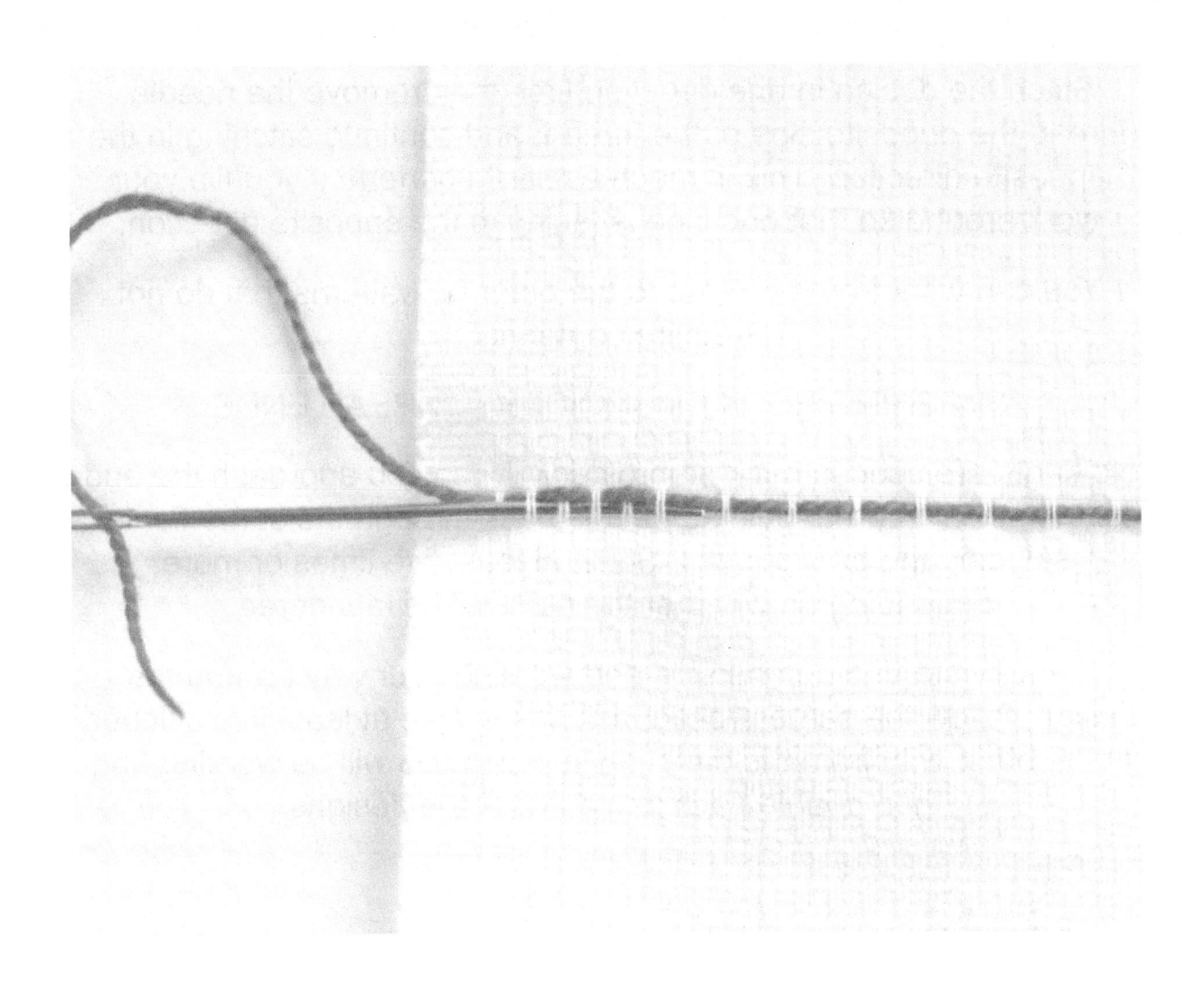

FOLLOWING THE HUCK EMBROIDERY PATTERN

In most cases, huck embroidery patterns are presented in one of two ways. Some are represented by gridded charts, while others are simply photographs with written notation and directions. With either pattern style, all you have to do is count the number of floats you want to stitch through or skip over, both horizontally and vertically.

Continue row after row, placing as many stitches onto the needle as comfortably fits or as the design permits. Simply ensure that only one row of floats is loaded at a time.

Certain rows will share floats with adjacent rows' stitches. Pass the needle through as you would for other rows, taking care not to pull too hard on the stitches or floats.

Pull the threads taut between each row of stitching, but not so tightly that the fabric puckers.

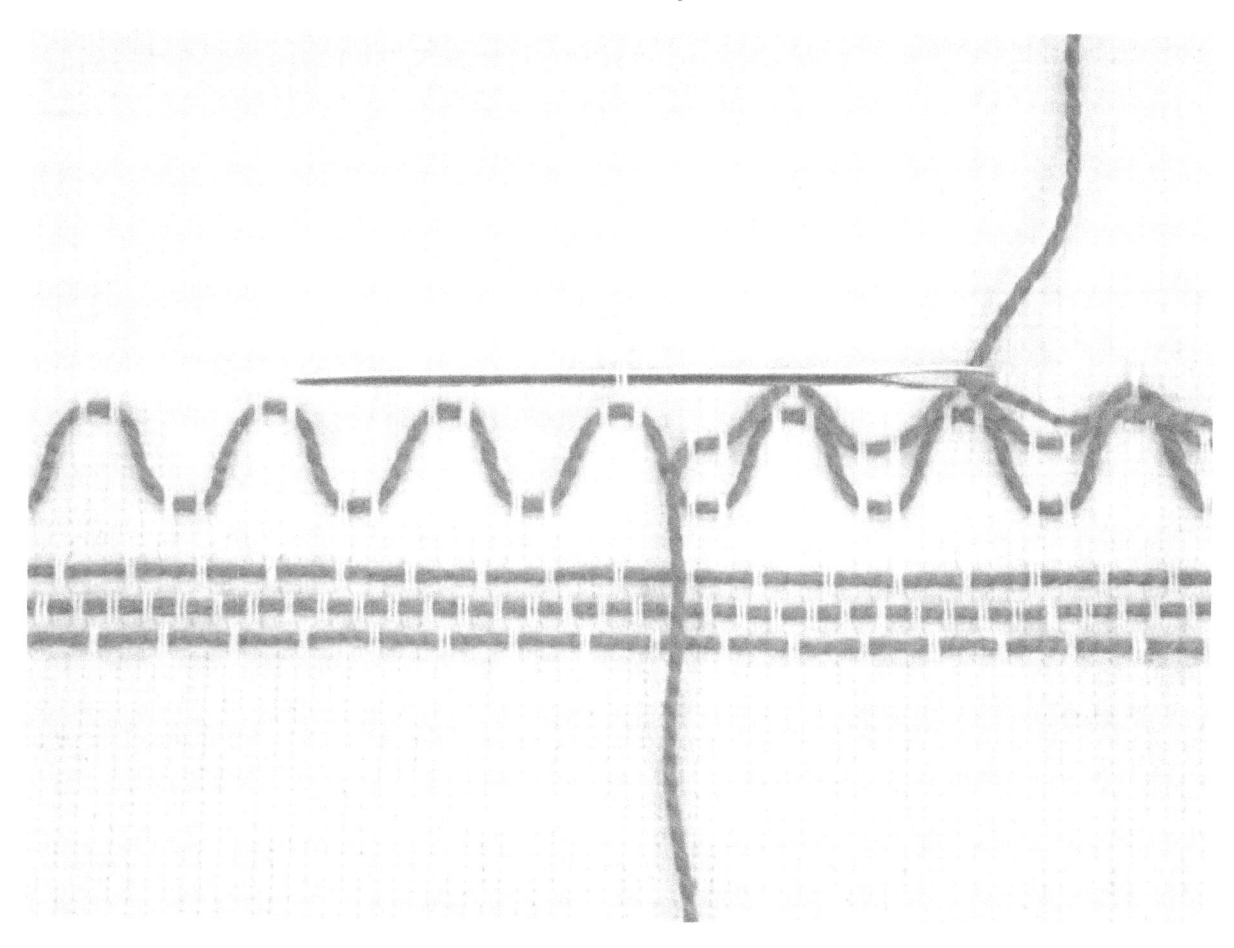

CREATE YOUR OWN HUCK DESIGN

Because huck stitching is so simple and straightforward, even a beginner may create improvised designs. Stitch a few straight lines (that appear to be running stitch!), then some zig-zags, and then a few more lines. Seek inspiration from other photographs of huck needlework.

To create the design pictured below or in the first image of this guide, use thread lengths that are 1-1/2 times the width of your fabric for straight rows and 2 times the width for curved or zig-zag rows.

These patterns are an excellent place to begin; then, look for more patterns and books to supplement your huck embroidery work.

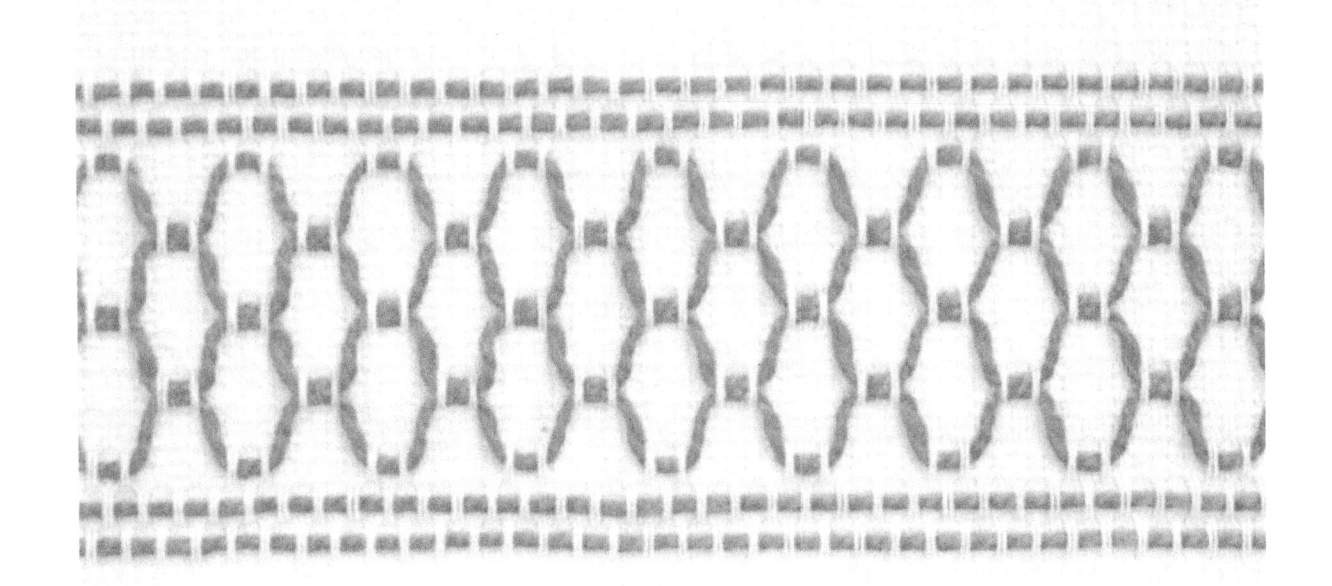

CHAPTER FIVE

DIY CANDLEWICK EMBROIDERY

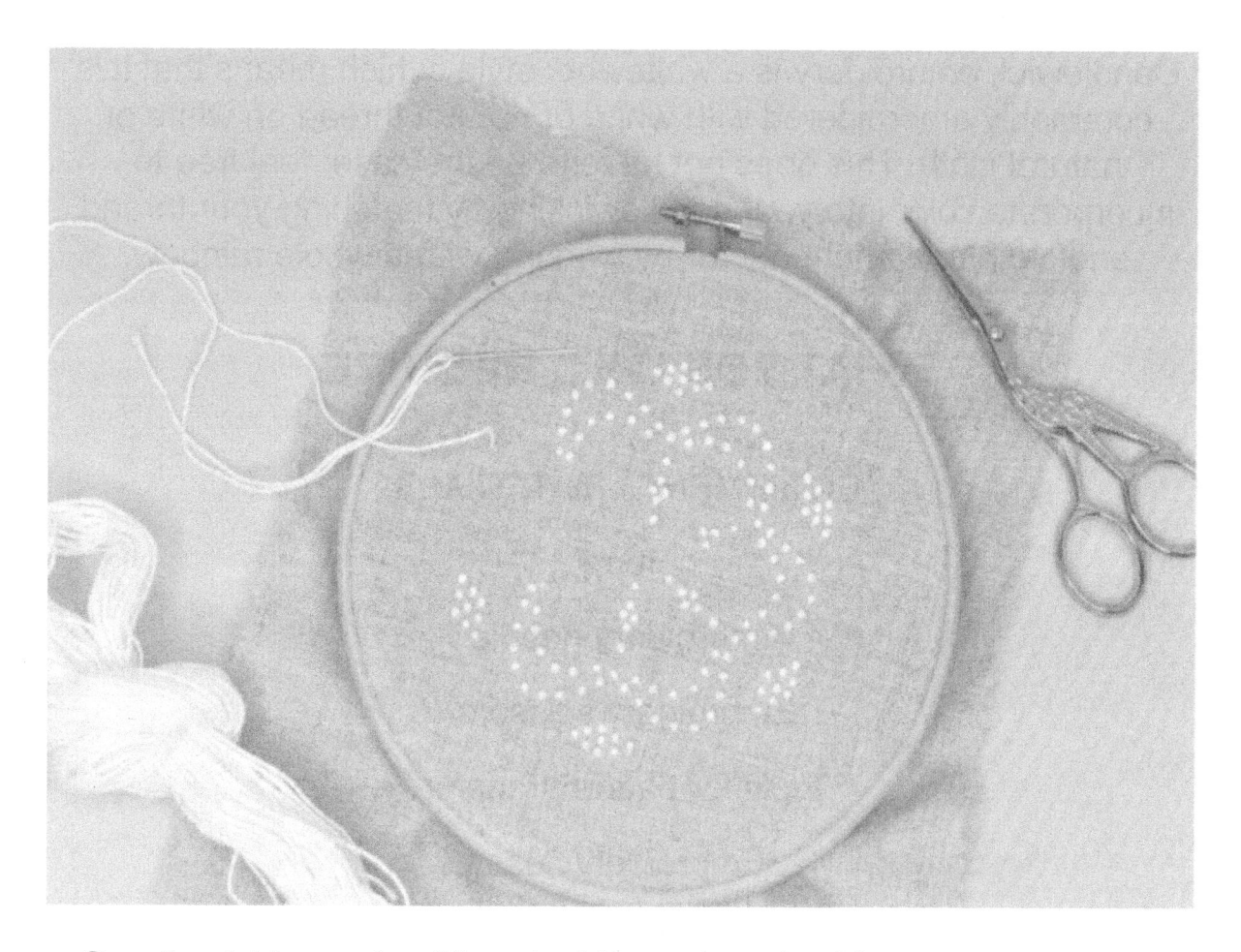

Candlewicking, a traditional whitework embroidery method, has a distinctive design that emphasizes Colonial knot stitches. In the early days of the United States, particularly during the Westward Expansion, fine embroidery threads were scarce—and certainly not practicable. However, due to the ease with which cotton threads for creating candle wicks could be obtained, they may have become the material of choice for those wishing to adorn quilts and other sewing items.

This embroidery style makes use of Colonial knots, which are tighter and more durable than their cousin, the French knot, making them ideal for usage on materials such as quilts that are subjected to a great deal of wear. Additionally, Colonial knots utilize significantly less thread than French knots. If supplies are limited, this is a significant selling point!

Candlewick embroidery is a whitework style, which means that it is commonly embroidered with white or natural thread on white or natural cloth. This does not have to be the case; feel free to incorporate color into your candlewicking by matching your thread and cloth to a bright hue or by working with a whole rainbow.

WHAT YOU WILL REQUIRE

EQUIPMENT / MATERIALS

Hoop

Embroidery needle

Embroidery scissors

Tools for pattern transfer

Embroidery floss

Fabric made of unbleached muslin or linen

INSTRUCTIONS

CONSTRUCT A COLONIAL KNOT

Begin by coming up through the fabric and then wrapping the working thread around the needle in a backward "C" shape.

BRING THE WORK THREAD OVER AND UNDER

Following that, bring the working thread over and under the needle's tip. The thread should have the appearance of a figure eight.

INSERT THE NEEDLE

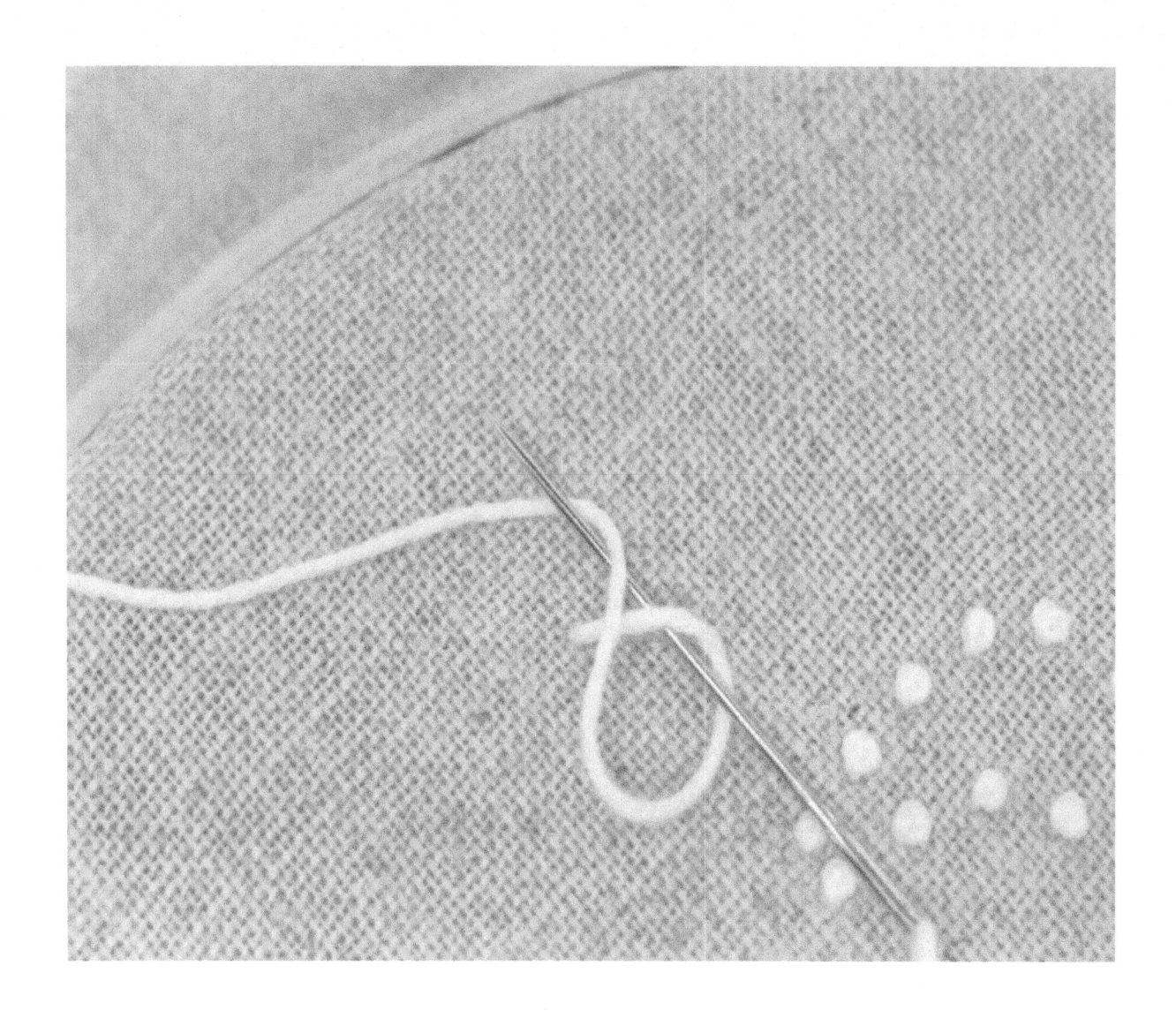

Insert the needle towards the beginning of the stitch in the fabric. You can return to the same hole; with looser-weave materials, this may cause the knot to pop through to the back. Tighten the knot around the needle by pulling on the working thread.

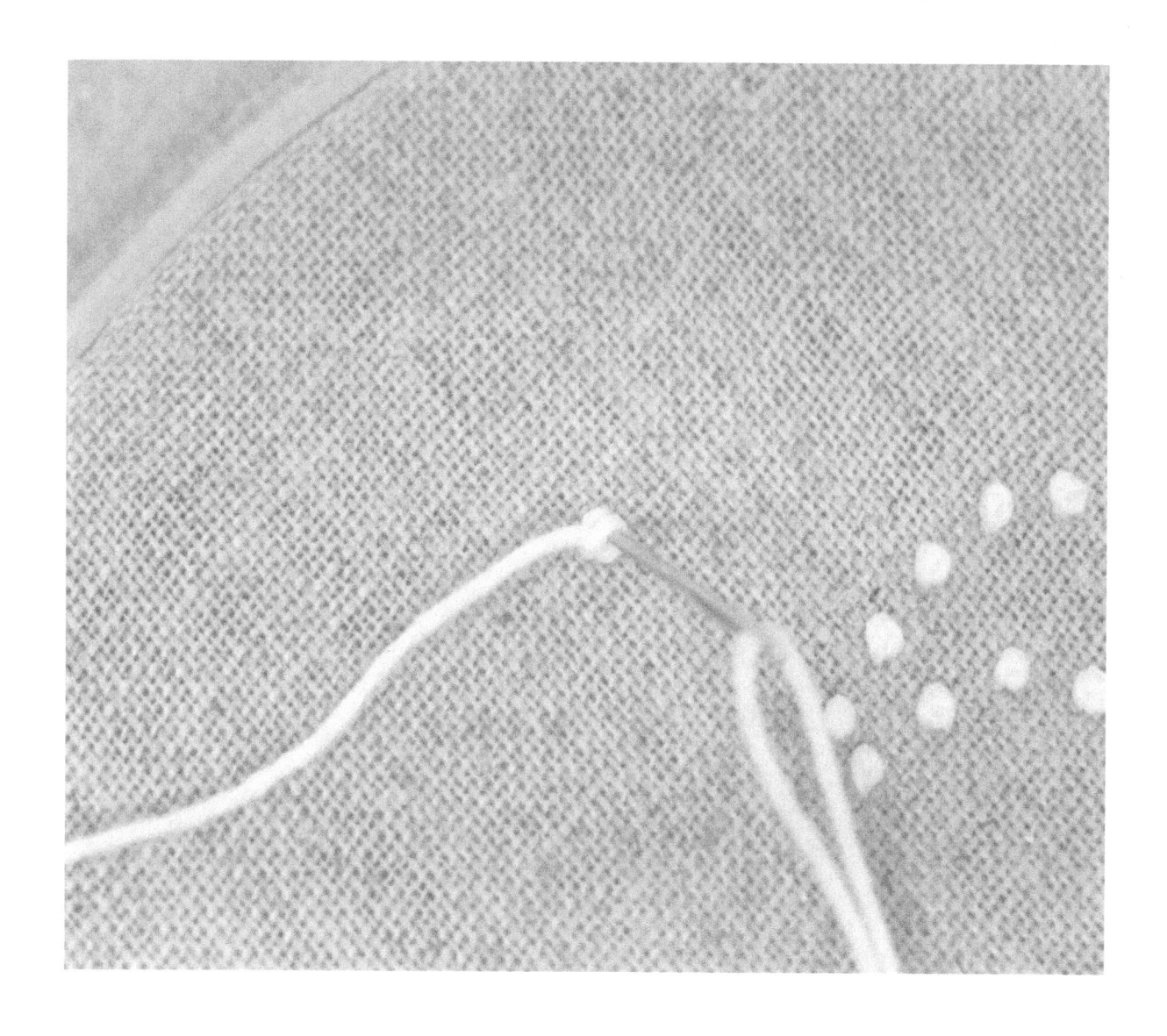

CREATE THE KNOT

Bring the needle and thread all the way through the fabric to form the knot, holding the working thread taut. Each Colonial knot should be worked in the same manner, ensuring that they are tight and consistent.

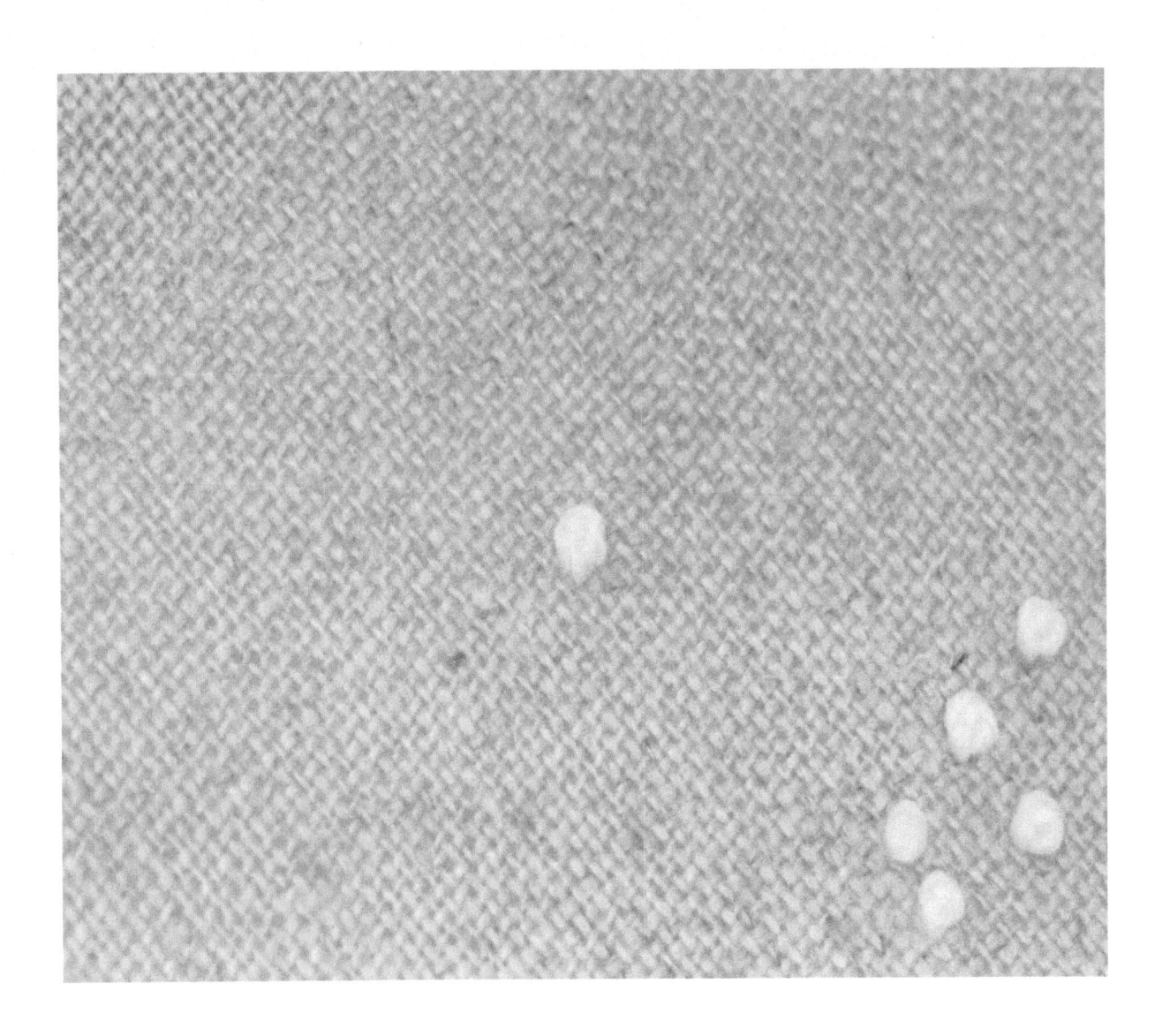

CANDLEWICK EMBROIDERY PATTERNS

There are numerous candlewick patterns available, including some that are free or are vintage transfers. Numerous designs are traditional in style and frequently use Colonial knots, back stitch, and occasional satin stitch. You can also utilize simple designs for standard embroidery and instead of an outline stitch, stitch the lines with a row of knots.

To begin, get this free candlewick embroidery design. It's a cross between a flower and a mandala, and stitching it is simple and enjoyable. Draw the pattern at a size of around 5 inches wide. Make a mark on your cloth with your preferred transfer method and set it in a hoop. To avoid tangling, work with sections of thread about the length of your elbow to the tips of your fingers.

Begin with a waste knot and weave in the ends afterwards, or just knot the thread's end and begin stitching. All that remains is to sew a Colonial knot on each dot in the pattern.

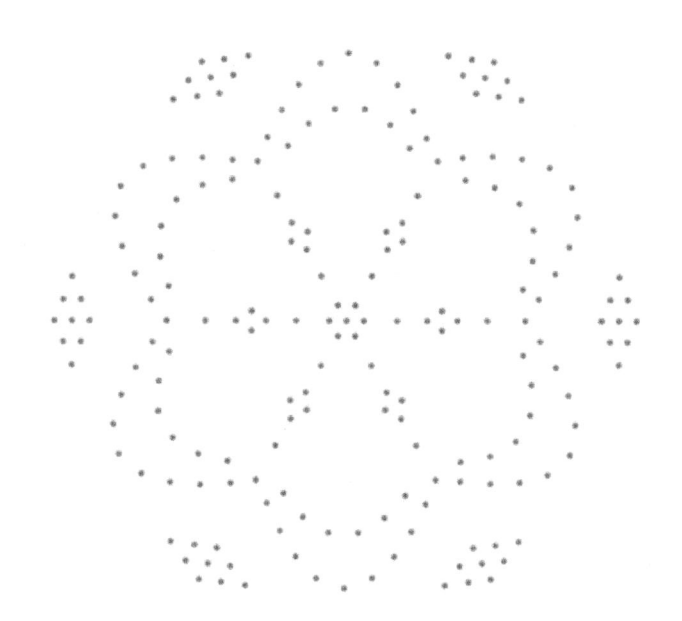

CHAPTER SIX

EMBROIDERED THROW PILLOW

The embroidered home sweet home throw pillow is easily customizable; however we chose the phrase "home sweet home" and used only two different stitches to keep the pillow looking simple and tidy.

SUPPLIES FOR THE EMBROIDERED THROW PILLOW

Throw pillow covers

Embroidery thread

Embroidery hoop

Needle

Embroidery pen

EMBROIDERED PILLOW: A STEP-BY-STEP TUTORIAL

DECIDE ON THE PHRASE

Decide on a phrase for your pillow and then write it out using the embroidery pen if you have good handwriting. If, like me, you have poor handwriting, you can enter the sentence in a typeface of your choice in a blank page. Then, you can use your computer as a light table by turning the brightness of your screen all the way up and placing your pillowcase on it. This allows you to view the lettering and trace it with your embroidery pen.

STICK THE EMBROIDERY HOOP

Insert the smaller of the two embroidery hoop circles into the pillowcase first, and then the larger round on top, encircling your first letter. Ensure that you are inside the pillowcase, or you will sew the entire case shut when you begin embroidering!

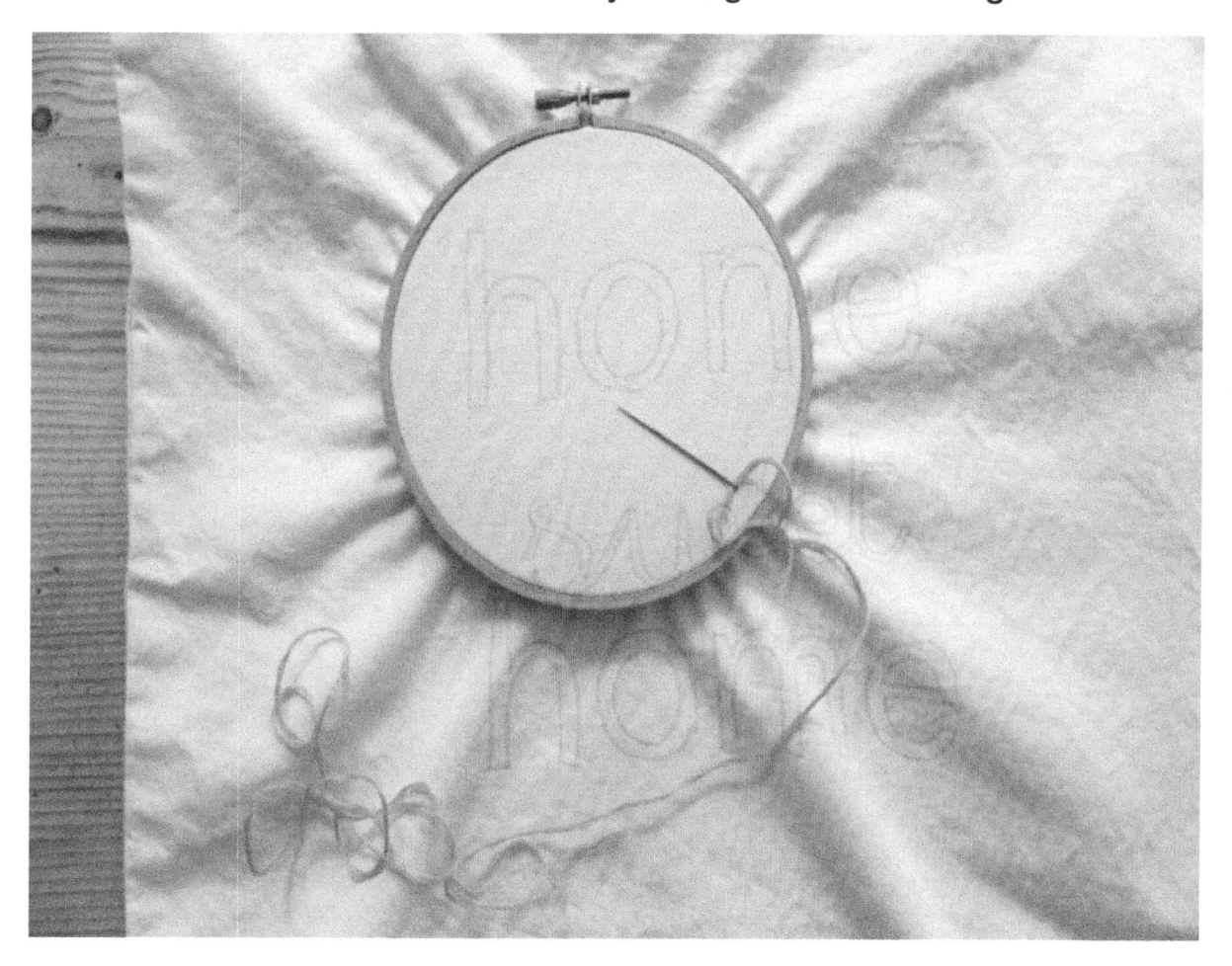

THREAD YOUR NEEDLE

Thread an embroidery thread through your needle and tie a knot at the end of the string. Poke the needle into the corner of your first letter, starting from the inside of the pillowcase, and then draw the needle and thread completely through. Reintroduce the needle and thread on the opposite corner of the letter's leg. Continue stitching back and forth across the letter until it is completely filled in.

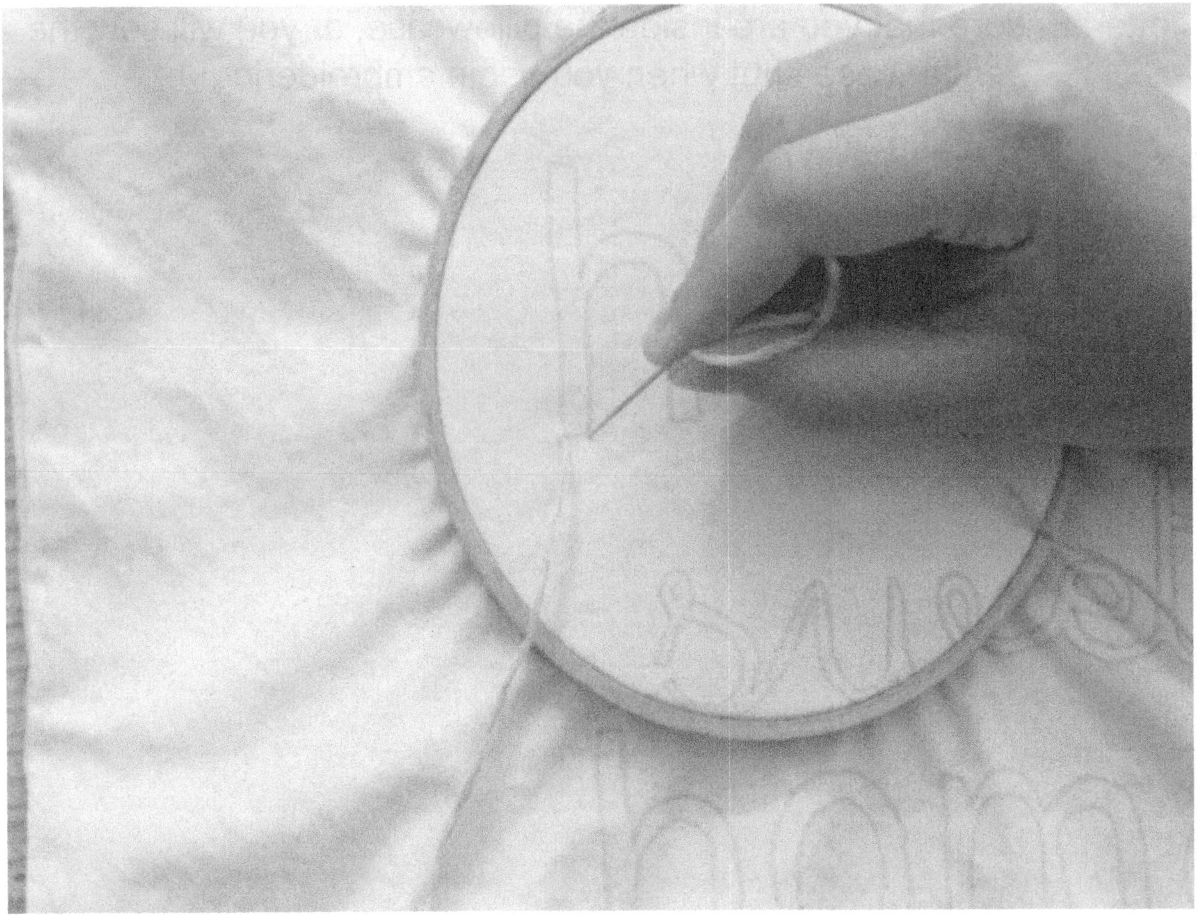

The cushion from the inside is shown below so you can see where to place your needle next:

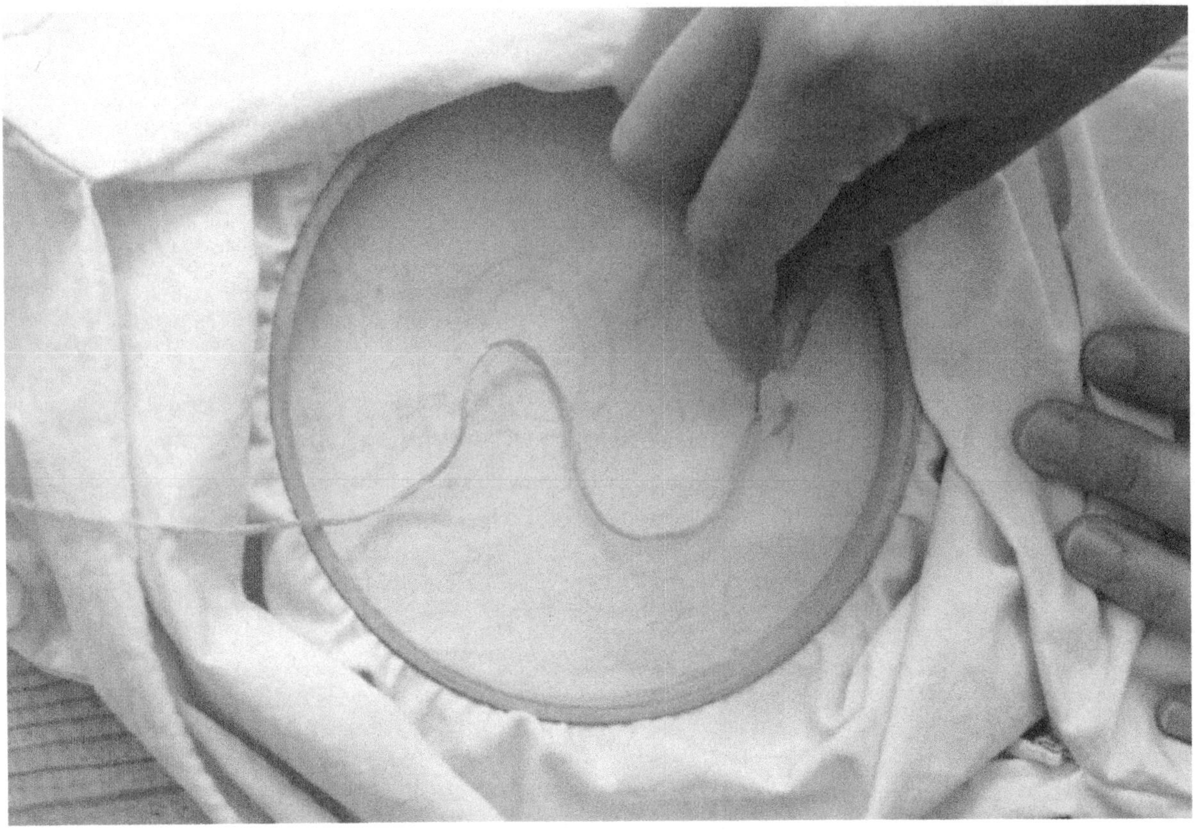

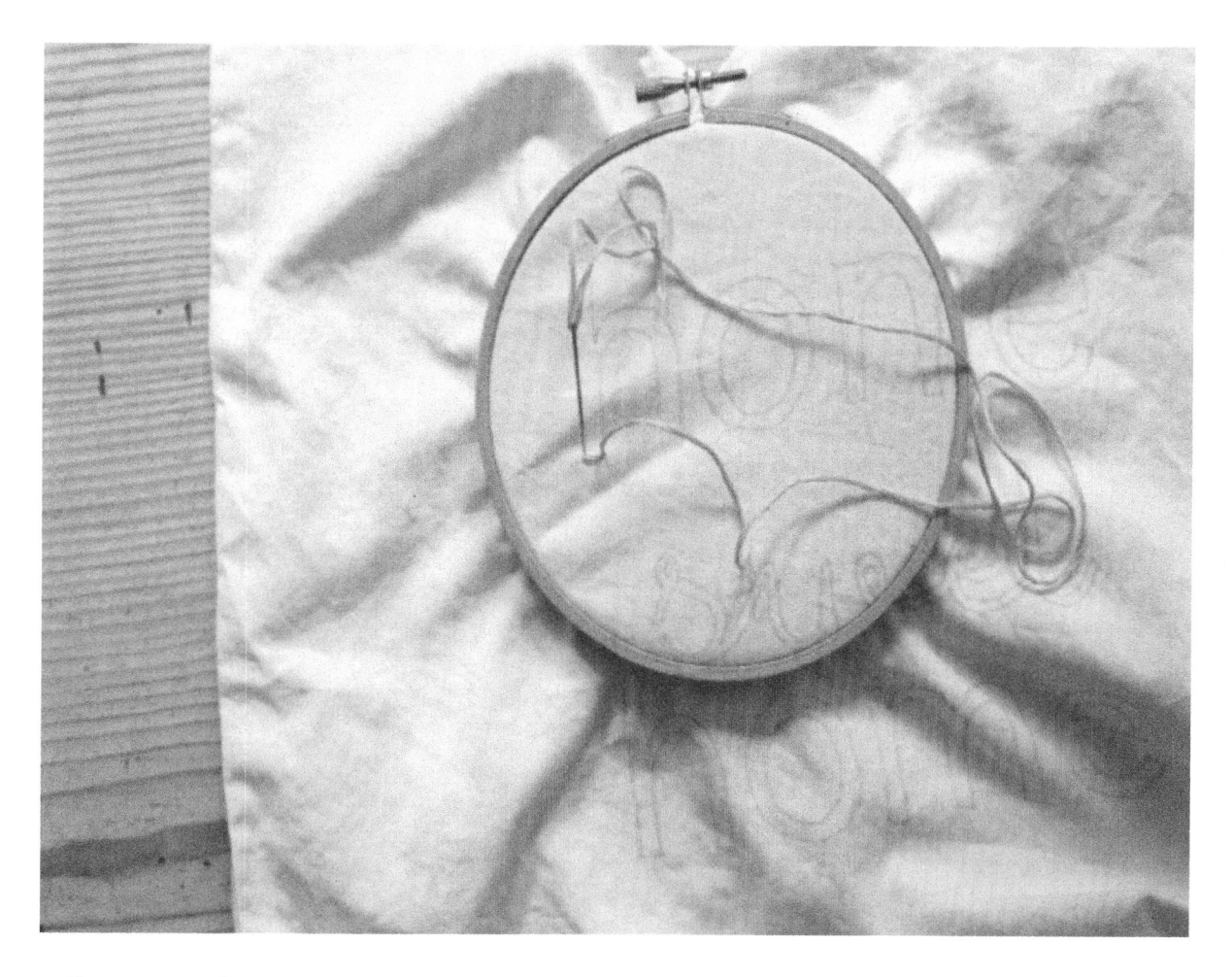

Once you're satisfied with your letter, tie it and move on to the next one. Continue in this manner until the entirety of your phrase is complete. We used a simple running stitch to sew the "sweet." To begin this, tie the knot and begin inside the pillowcase, just as you did previously. Continue stitching in and out along the words online until you reach the beginning.

At last, I've arrived! Because I don't do much stitching, I wanted to share something that was simple enough for anyone to make yet still looked great. This craft is quite enjoyable

CHAPTER SEVEN

DIY EMBROIDERED MAGNETS

I enjoy hand stitching, but I always struggle to come up with practical uses for my hand embroidery designs. I decided to make some DIY magnets containing some stitched small embroidered flowers, and they ended out really gorgeous! I've included some free flower embroidery patterns for you, but if you're not familiar with embroidery, that's fine. You may also construct these DIY magnets out of lovely fabric or vintage embroidery pieces.

MATERIALS

Kit of 1-1/8 inch cover buttons and 1-1/8 inch cover buttons

Pliers

Magnets

Strong glue

Embroidery hoop

Fabric that is woven (cotton or linen)

Embroidery floss

Needle

Carbon paper

GUIDELINES

Transfer one of the flower embroidery patterns on a piece of fabric by cutting it. I enjoy using carbon paper that I purchased at a fabric store. Simply trace over it and the design is transferred to the fabric by the pressure.

Create embroidery designs for your flowers. If you need assistance with the stitches, you can check other books or check the web on how to embroidery stitches. It's not nearly as difficult as it appears, I assure you! Due to the small size of these, I used only one strand of floss.

Take your cover button kit and trace a larger circle around your design using the template. Remove the circle.

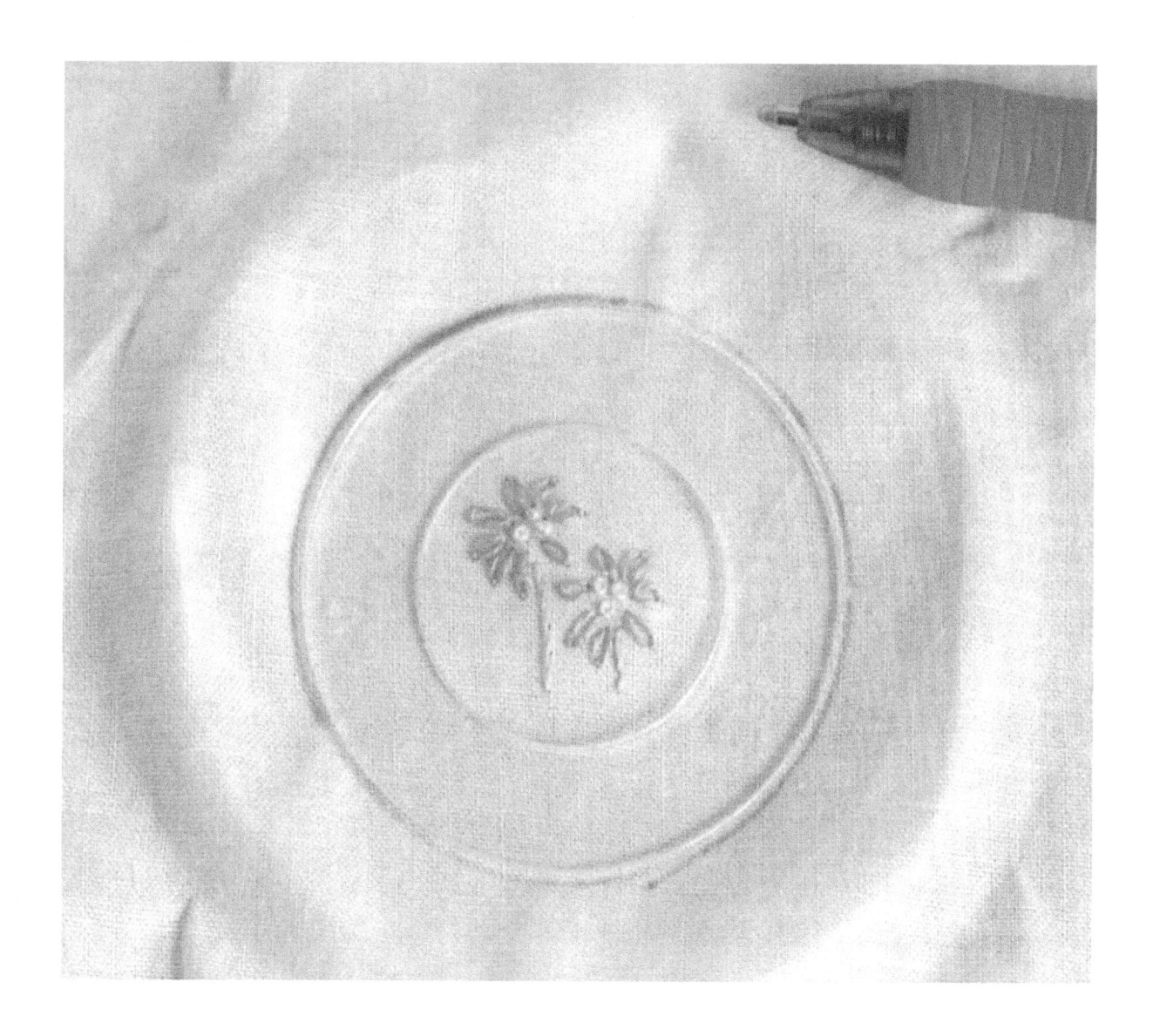

Some of my buttons featured just plain backs, while others included shank backs (like the photo below). If you have a choice, opt for simple backs to avoid this step. If your buttons have a shank back, bend and pull out the shank using pliers. If the surface is uneven due to the holes, use the pliers to press down on any protruding metal. This creates a smooth surface for later sticking the magnets.

Assemble your button according to the instructions placed on the kit. Place the fabric face down in the kit, followed by the button, which should be pressed down with the presser. This is how it should seem. If the flower embroidery pattern does not end up being centered, disassemble everything and try again.

Fold the excess fabric into the button's center and place the button's back on top. Again, use the presser to secure everything, and the back will spring into place.

It is vital that you use magnets that are neither too strong nor too weak. I once created magnets that were so strong that they detached from the glue to stick to the refrigerator. That is not what you desire! The magnets I purchased were from a well recommended craft store and rated a 7 out of 10. I'm not sure what that means, but my magnets have been performing admirably thus far! Additionally, you'll need some decent, strong glue.

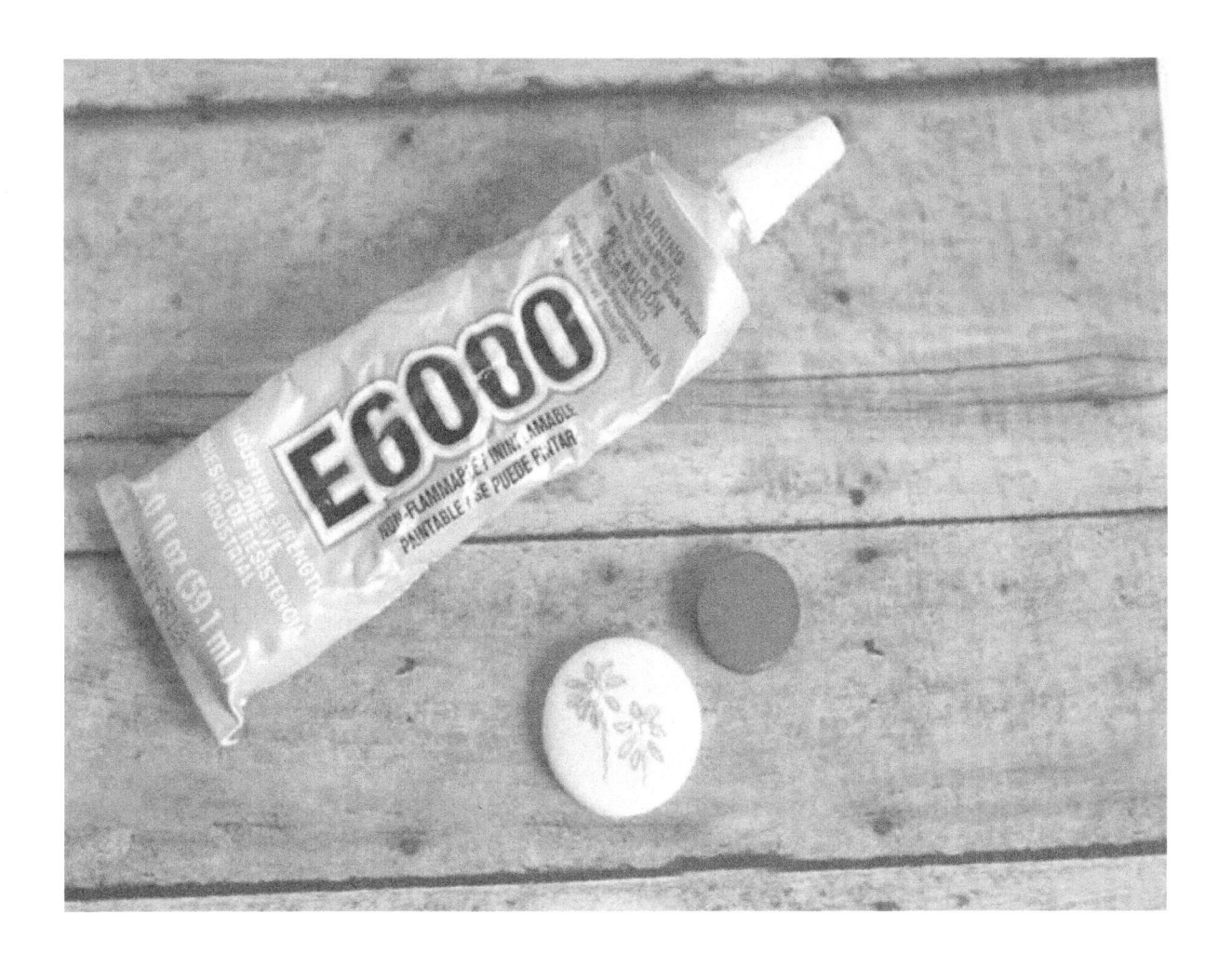

Attach a magnet to the back of each button and allow it dry completely. Avoid leaving them too near together when drying, or the magnets will begin to migrate in the same direction. Inquire as to how I know.

That is all! I'm in love with my new homemade magnets. They look stunning on my refrigerator and are ideal for spring!

Made in the USA
Coppell, TX
08 December 2024